CONSUMING FOOTBALL IN LATE MODERN LIFE

To 'wor Jack'.

Consuming Football in Late Modern Life

KEVIN DIXON
Teesside University, UK

Routledge
Taylor & Francis Group

LONDON AND NEW YORK

First published 2013 by Ashgate Publishing

2 Park Square, Milton Park, Abingdon, Oxfordshire OX14 4RN
52 Vanderbilt Avenue, New York, NY 10017

Routledge is an imprint of the Taylor & Francis Group, an informa business

First issued in paperback 2019

British Library Cataloguing in Publication Data
A catalogue record for this book is available from the British Library

The Library of Congress has cataloged the printed edition as follows:
Dixon, Kevin.
  Consuming football in late modern life / by Kevin Dixon.
    pages cm
  Includes bibliographical references and index.
  ISBN 978-1-4094-5094-8 (hardback)
  1. Soccer. 2. Soccer--Economic aspects. 3. Consumption (Economics) I. Title.
  GV943.D54 2013
  796.334--dc23

2013000251

ISBN 978-1-4094-5094-8 (hbk)
ISBN 978-0-367-33294-5 (pbk)

Contents

Acknowledgements

I would like to thank Professor Ellis Cashmore for his constructive advice through the process of writing this book. I would extend my appreciation to Dr. Philip Whitehead, Dr. Paul Crawshaw, Dr. Tom Gibbons, Stuart Braye, Mike McGuinness, Dr. Anne Lodge and Dr. Darren Flynn for taking the time to discuss ideas. Finally, in the course of writing this book, I thank the team at Ashgate for seeing this project through, and of course, I thank my parents for their invaluable support.

Chapter 1
Introduction: Everyday Fandom as Consumption

Bill: I'm not a fanatic by any means but football is part of my daily existence. It is the clothes I wear and its part of me ... lots of stuff in my house relates to Sunderland. The colour scheme, the wall paper in one room, I've got Sunderland cups and saucers. That sort of stuff ... Early in the week I'm talking about football. I go on internet forums as well to chat about the previous match ... By Wednesday, I'm looking ahead to the next match ... I buy papers and watch TV shows; basically I'm always doing something related to Sunderland. Most matches, I watch on Sky (Sky television), sometimes with my mates and a shit load of food and drink. This is the highlight of my week ... Winning puts a prolonged smile on my face; losing makes the week ahead tough, but yeah, the shirt, the badge and the team are a major part of my life. They will go with me to the grave. [Sunderland, aged 34]

For Bill and millions of others like him, football[1] fandom practice occurs primarily through routine acts of consumption. In his contextual self appraisal of the everyday fandom experience (above), 'Bill' inadvertently describes how consumption infiltrates every level of practice[2] to such an extent that affiliation to football is impossible without it. After all, choice of clothing; food; television shows; interior decoration; emotional labour; online activities and general sociability, are all, in the end, acts of consumption, or by-products of consumption acts. Even live televised viewing of 'the match' (emphasised by Bill as the highlight of his week), when scrutinised more closely comprises many other consumption acts that exist in the space between buying the television set and licence; sports channels; food; beverages; other match accompaniments; and watching/preparing for the match per se. In other words, to practice is to consume, not only in a monetary or utilitarian sense, but it also serves to convey a way of thinking, with agents spending money, time and part of themselves on football.

---

1 The term 'football' is used throughout this book to refer to the sport of Association Football, often abbreviated to 'soccer'.

2 During the course of this book the term 'practice' refers to the performance of conduct and interactions between football fans.

Notwithstanding the logic portrayed above, the question of whether association football fans can be defined as consumers remains a contentious one within the sociological literature. Whilst it has not gone unnoticed that football has reaped the benefits of commercial enterprise (Giulianotti 1999, 2002, Horne 2006, King 1998, Manzenreiter and Horne 2004) there remains a stubborn denial that 'real fans' of football can be labelled as consumers at all. Instead, scholars have tended to preserve romanticised notions of fandom orthodoxy, often positioning 'fans' and 'consumers' at opposing ends of a hypothetical dichotomy that downgrades certain consumer activities (for example, buying merchandise, replica shirts, partaking in virtual communications) and celebrates forms of perceived 'traditional loyalty' (for example, attending football matches in person). The problem with such distinctions, of course, is that perceived traditional acts (for example, match attendance) require fans to consume in multiple ways. Most obviously, they must buy tickets and spend time and money at the stadium or in the stadium vicinity. In addition to this, it is not inconceivable to suggest that those attending the stadium may also buy merchandise and take part in other consumption activities such as watching football on television or contributing to internet discussions about football.

Consequently, value laden distinctions of this type are largely unhelpful to the sociology of football in the sense that they form rigid divisions between mythical groupings and place types of behaviour into restrictive and ultimately unrealistic categories (Crawford 2004, 2007, Dixon 2011, Gibbons and Dixon 2010). In an attempt to avoid false dichotomies of this nature and to acknowledge the fluidity of fandom practice, no such distinctions are made during the course of this book. Instead, it is argued that the terms 'consumers' and 'fans' ought to be used interchangeably given that the manner of affiliation to football must ultimately occur through acts of consumption. Accordingly then, the reader of this book is encouraged to visualise fans of football as both products and constituents of a culture in which consumption is of paramount importance.

Though this is a book about consumption, it does not solely refer to the action of economic exchange. After all, apart from consumption's frequent and often explicit economic properties, it can be partially, if not entirely, 'experiential' (Watts 1999, Bourdieu 2002, Falk 2007). For the seller of course, customer consumption is a means to an end, but for the consumer, acts of consumption are much more than this. They can hold (or are attributed by the customer) intrinsic value, surpassing the economic and extending import beyond installed meanings at the point of production (Sayer 1997). This has implications for our understanding of consumer behaviour, with utilitarian and economic aspects of consumption, conceivably less significant to the consumer experience overall. Consequently, it is possible to acknowledge the presence of a 'consumer mentality' that is 'orientated toward the realm of representations rather than mere need satisfaction' (Falk 2007: 716). So, whilst experiential aspects of consumption have been used to explain the motives for and desired outcomes of economic expenditure (Veblen 1925, Bourdieu 1984, Willis 1990, McCraken 1991, Campbell 1995, Ilmonen 2004, Warde 2005, Horne 2006, Bauman 2007a, Illouz 2009), scholars now recognise the place and importance of the experiential component as a defining constituent of consumption per se. This is typified by Warde (2005: 137) when he writes:

> [consumption is] … a process whereby agents engage in appropriation and appreciation, whether for utilitarian, expressive or contemplative purposes, of goods, services, performances, information or ambience, whether purchased or not, over which the agent has some degree of discretion.

It is clear then, that scholars largely support the position that consumption can infiltrate practice at experiential as well as purely economic levels, and in relation to football fandom, I argue that fandom studies would benefit if linked more closely to wider issues of everyday life and to consumer culture more specifically. In agreement with this, Gray et al. (2007: 8) encourage researchers to acknowledge the advancing technological modes of consumption that 'extend the prospect of engaging in fan activities' and reflect 'the increasing entrenchment of fan consumption in the structure of our everyday life'. Likewise, Horne (2006: 11) acknowledges the entrenchment of consumption, and consequently raises the following point. He argues that scholars of sport ought to investigate 'the real world of consumption' on the premise that 'most consumption is probably mundane, routine and inconspicuous'. Hence, it is precisely because fan consumption has grown as a taken for granted aspect of late modern life that it warrants critical analysis and investigation now more than ever (Crawford 2004, Horne 2006, Gray, Sandvoss and Harrington 2007). Still, in spite of this admission from the research field, a paucity of research activity has placed 'ordinary' fandom practice (that is, routine experiential and material consumption) under empirical scrutiny, and subsequently fandom remains profoundly under theorised:

> Although we use the term with abandon, fans and their social and cultural environment ("fandom") are profoundly untheorised in the social sciences. We know virtually nothing about what produces fandom, what specific practices are associated with it [and] what role fans may play in social and cultural processes. (Harris 1998: 4)

Following the logic set out above, this book locates discussions of football fan cultures within the sociology of consumption in order to develop an empirically based, theoretical account of football fandom in late modern life. In doing so it contributes to the development of a critical sociology that raises the profile of everyday consumption experiences and indicates the significance of these in the construction, maintenance and evolution of football fandom cultures.

The Research Process

Before providing more details of the arguments derived from this investigation, it is useful at the outset, to briefly explain the research undertaken. In response to recent calls for empirical, rather than conceptually based work relating to football fandom (Stone 2007, Williams 2007, Gibbons and Dixon 2010) a sample of football fans were interviewed during the course of this work. Interviews were semi-structured, allowing respondents to discuss open-ended questions and aiding the researcher to explore in more depth, understandings of football fandom practice from those directly implicated (Silverman 2000, Hoffman 2007). Furthermore, in accordance with Witzel (2000), an interview guide encompassing areas of interest was used to offer a sense of continuity within and between interviews, without adhering rigidly to a strict line of questioning.

The interview guide consisted of two general principles. First, it aimed to explore the genesis of football fandom under the assumption that this would offer a central reference point from which fandom behaviour has developed for participants. This follows Weber (1968: 18) who explains that any 'real empirical sociological investigation begins with the question: what motives determine and lead individual members ... in this socialistic community to behave in such a way that the community came into being in the first place, and that it continues to exist'. In the case of football fandom, this is an under researched area that has potential to hold some crucial information, not only relating to the genesis of fandom, but it also offers a foundation from which to explore the development of fandom cultures over time (Crawford 2004). Secondly, given that a key aim of this book was to explore and explain the everyday lived experiences of football fandom; then 'routine' elements of fandom practice were discussed with all participants. It was decided that free-flowing, naturalistic discourse regarding the experiences of football fandom would yield contextually rich and less contrived information for subsequent analysis (Alasuutari 1995). Interviews took place over a seven month period between August 2008 and February 2009.

Recruitment Strategy and Participant Information

Participants were recruited from the North-East region of England. This region is often referred to as 'the hotbed of football', a tag that was first used in the 1961 Arthur Appleton book of the same name. As the title implies, football culture is thought to be particularly strong in the North East, this is in spite of the relative mediocrity of the teams representing this region (in terms of recent [last 50 years] League success). Within the North East of England there are five professional football teams at different levels of the football pyramid. In 2008-09 (the same season as data collection) those teams were positioned in the following English leagues: *(Premier League)* Sunderland; Newcastle United; Middlesbrough; *(Football League 1)* Hartlepool United; *(Football League 2)* Darlington – though it should be noted that at the end of season 2008-09 both Newcastle United and Middlesbrough were relegated from The Premier League into the Championship.

To obtain a body of potential participants, a University press release was launched in 2008 with a number of local media outlets responding. Media exposure afforded the researcher an opportunity to publicise the research and canvas for volunteers.[3] With each exposure, contact details of the researcher were publicised and interested parties were encouraged to make contact. On acknowledgement of interest, volunteers were selected as participants for subsequent interview according to the following criteria: (1) Given that scholars Malcolm, Jones and Waddington (2000) acknowledge season ticket holders as most frequently and disproportionately used within academic literature to represent all fans; the inclusion of fandom narratives from a wider range of experiential profiles was selected. This is particularly important in the current context in order to illustrate everyday experiences of fandom within and beyond the football stadium. (2) It was deemed important not to privilege fans of top tier teams (for example, Manchester United, Chelsea, and Arsenal) over and above the majority of fans that support teams outside of this elite group. This has been a common characteristic within recent academic research where authors such as King (1998) and, additionally, Sandvoss (2003) have studied fans of a handful of top tier clubs in their domestic leagues. (3) Finally, on the recommendations of Jones (2008) I agree that it was important to be inclusive of female fans and also to take into account a range of age groups.

Sixty football fans (36 male and 24 female [aged 18-56]) were interviewed during the course of this investigation. Of those participants, thirty were current season ticket holders. The remaining thirty were not current holders of season tickets at the time of interview, although they did watch or listen to live football multiple times per-week via the media. Therefore, for the purpose of transparency within the transcript extracts and *not for the purpose of systematic*

---

3 Following the launch of a University Press Release, the following media outlets in the North East of England gave time and column inches to promote the research: Newspapers: *The Journal; The Northern Echo; Hartlepool Mail; The Sunderland Echo; Evening Gazette; Newcastle Evening Chronicle*. Television: *BBC North East News; ITV North East Tonight*. Radio Interviews: *Durham FM 102.6; Century Radio 106 (now 'Real Radio'); BBC Tees – The Neil Green Show; The Matthew Davies Breakfast Show; The Chris Johnson Show*.

comparison, they are identified as: (1) Season Ticket Holders (STH); (2) Media Fans (MF), to reflect their primary mode of live football consumption at the time of the interview. It is worth emphasising that this *was not* an attempt to categorise fans into a simplistic dichotomy representative of fandom type. Rather, sharing the belief that fandom can be a fluid process across one's life cycle (Crawford 2004), such labels are used solely to provide further information for the reader regarding the current (but not permanent) status of live match consumption in relation to participants.

In terms of supported teams, 51 participants were fans of one of the following 2008 English Premier League Clubs: Newcastle (N=18); Middlesbrough (N=18); Sunderland (N=12); Liverpool (N=2) and West Ham (N=1). Of the remaining participants, nine were supporters of one of the following teams: Hartlepool (N=5) and Darlington (N=4). Key characteristics of this sample are shown below.

Table 1.1   Key Characteristics of the Sample

Key characteristics of the sample	Number	Percentage
Male	36	60
Female	24	40
Age		
19-29	32	53
30-39	11	18
40-49	11	18
50-59	6	10
Premier League fans	51	85
Lower Division fans	9	15
Season Ticket Holders (STH)	30	50
Media Fans (MF)	30	50

During the course of this book evidence gathered from interview transcriptions is used verbatim (that is, changing the name of the participant, but presenting all other demographic information) to instantiate points of view, substantiate an argument or to provide support for a crucial point. Whilst the work is instantiated with individual accounts, it offers more than an individual appraisal of football fandom. Like Weber (1968: 18) suggests, it would be 'a tremendous misunderstanding to think that individualist method should involve what is in any conceivable sense an individualistic system of values'. Rather, those patterns and regularities that are discernible through practice are the consequences of learned meanings and thus, narratives presented during the course of this book offer a thorough and accurate description of the range of opinions, experiences and reactions that were expressed throughout the research process.

Structure and Organisation of this Book

This book is divided into seven chapters inclusive of this introduction. Chapter 2 sets a historical background to the work by emphasising the point that consumption for football fans is not simply a new, late modern phenomenon. Drawing on newsprint extracts from national newspapers of the day, and the work of sport historians, this chapter illustrates the rise of football fandom as consumption. Amongst other developments it illuminates the importance of industry and the aligned trade union movement of the late nineteenth century by detailing its contribution to the genesis of consumer culture and to the development of spectator sport. Furthermore, the emergence of football cultures is discussed in relation to their capacity for representativeness, not only of team, but also of geographical localities. Those factors are considered in line with the growth and commercial potential of the practice from the early- to mid-twentieth century. In contrast, the latter part of this chapter deals with the subsequent demise of spectator football from the mid- to late-twentieth century, closely followed with brief discussions of the subsequent rebuilding and re-branding of football for the late modern period. The issues raised here are important, not only to provide context for discussions that occur in Chapters 4-7, but also to recognise the historical basis from which previous sociological theories relating to football fandom have developed.

Chapter 3 draws together past and current theoretical explanations of football fandom practice with particular reference to the much contested sociological debate that tends to situate fandom as either a direct descendent of social structure or alternatively a process that is shaped and designed by individuals. It explains how those diverse theoretical positions have ultimately served to create unrealistic theoretical dichotomies or typologies as explanations for football fandom practice and argues instead that a new theoretical perspective is warranted in order to more accurately depict the nature of fandom in the late modern period. With criticisms cast against macro and micro paradigms it is suggested that meso level theories may best solve the theoretical problems identified.

Chapter 4 is the first of three to present findings from the analysis of primary data. It begins by drawing attention to underpinning forms of experiential consumption that contribute towards the genesis of football fandom culture. This sets the scene by articulating the various means through which fandom is learned, adopted and consequently practiced. The influence of peer and kin groups are discussed with reference to (amongst other theorists) Bourdieu's (1984) theory of practice. Trends that exist outside of this framework are explained in light of late modern life, with particular reference to Peterson's (1992) concept of the cultural omnivore.

Chapter 5 looks beyond the consequences of engagement within football culture to illustrate the omnipresence of corporate consumer logic. It makes particular reference to corporate inflections to demonstrate that those processes have, over time, become ingrained into many aspects of football fandom culture. Consequently, it draws upon Bryman's (2004) concept of Disneyisation as a means of explaining this process at work and suggests that football fandom cultures have evolved to become infused with the values of the market which they subsume in practice.

Chapter 6 explores the routine manner through which football fandom culture is practiced. It explains away the more mundane elements of consumption that are often neglected in other academic works and it places a strong emphasis on the importance of the sociability of football to the generality of social conduct. Thus, the security that participants glean from the repetitive nature of seemingly trivial, mundane, routinised consumption behaviours is acknowledged as a central and yet under reported component of football fandom culture. Notwithstanding the stability gathered from routine consumption practice, this chapter also draws attention to the simultaneous, and yet subtle evolution of football fandom cultures over time. Thus, the rise of new technologies when combined with those Disneyisation properties (disclosed in Chapter 5) are discussed in relation to a practice that is continuously changing and moving boundaries of authenticity.

Chapter 7 draws a conclusion to this book by recalling those objectives set out at the start and demonstrating how they have been fulfilled by the analysis. Moreover, it offers a new theoretical outlook for football fandom in late modern life that steers between and merges existing theoretical perspectives. In doing so, the work demonstrates that football fandom cannot be explained by structural conditions or individual choice alone. It is argued that football fandom culture is part of an organic process of change that is communicated, maintained and altered through acts of consumption.

Chapter 2
Football Fandom as Consumption: A Historical Perspective

When discussing football fandom it is often assumed that the presence of consumption and thus 'the consumer fan' is a late modern phenomenon that is taking the game away from its 'innocent past'. In this sense, fandom is perceived and plotted on a degenerative continuum across time and space, invoking clear dividing lines between generations and traditions of fandom. As a typical instance, journalists such as A. Hubbard (*The Guardian* 1997[1]) suggest that 'those who run the game don't appear to give a toss about the fan in the street' or those 'who supported football before it became a fat cat industry'. Similarly, journalist Hunter Davies (*The Guardian* 1995[2]) regresses to a period 'once upon a time', where 'football was about glory, loyalty and local identity'. This, he claims, 'is a thing of the past', with clubs set to abandon fans in favour of 'the relentless pursuit of profit'. In support of those journalistic articles, books such as Ed Horton's (1997) aptly entitled *Moving the Goalposts: Football's Exploitation*, have given life to accusations that there exists a 'traditional' type of fan. Moreover traditional fans, he insists, are rapidly being replaced by new, affluent 'consumer' fans. Horton (1997: 27) maintains that 'football is no longer about ... traditional supporters', but instead it is about 'selling a product' and consequently, he claims that football is increasingly becoming a game for consumers. Similar arguments are made by authors David Conn (1997), Stephen Morrow (1999) and Craig McGill (2001) in relation to football's business model. All authors (cited above) emphasise the point that traditional fans (though the necessary and sufficient conditions of this categorisation remain unclear) are losing out in the face of a relatively new phenomenon within this practice – 'capitalist exploitation'.

In this chapter I challenge the notion above, arguing instead that writers (that is, those cited above) have not fully understood the continuity that exists across time and space in relation to consumption. When scholars talk of a romanticised golden period where fans were not exploited as consumers, I suggest that this period did not really exist in the manner that the authors propose. To be clear,

---

1 Hubbard, A. 1997. 'A game too big for its boots'. *The Guardian*, January. 19:7.
2 Davies, H. 1995. 'A new set of goals'. *The Guardian*, April 4:2.

I am not arguing that the Football Association, The Football League, or indeed individual football clubs were always profit maximisers in the true commercial sense, motivated by an unquenchable thirst to extract surplus cash from supporters, advertisers, and the media. After all there is evidence to the contrary (Sloane 1971, Vamplew 1988, Holt 1990, Russell 1997, Szymanski and Kuypers 1999, Taylor 2008). However, I do suggest that football is part of a wider story that is entwined with the commercial enlightenment. For instance, I argue that from the late nineteenth century onwards, football fans have been cultivated so that they were not just spectators, but they were consumers as well. Once the conditions (favourable for the market to thrive) were in place, entrepreneurs from all sectors of the economy (including those originally unconnected to football) saw the potential of spectator football as a means for enhancing profits, and thus, the nascent market began to take shape. I argue that football fans were always consumers; but where this was initially minimal and concealed to the naked eye – now, in late modern life it is simply 'naked'. I make this point (below) by examining the history of a society that has helped to create and sustain football fandom cultures in England, and I begin by outlining the rise of leisure consumption.

Association Football and the Rise of Leisure Consumption

According to Brailsford (1991) and Bennett (2005), the most important factor and instrumental influence with regard to the genesis of consumer culture was the rise of the trade union movement in the early nineteenth century. This was vital in the sense that the representation and subsequent pressure of workers' unions led to the initiation of government statutes that were, in turn, crucial to the evolution of leisure in the United Kingdom. They include: The Factories Act of 1847 (also known as The Ten Hours Act), freeing workers on Saturdays for the pursuit of leisure; the Reform Acts of 1867 and 1884, extending this franchise to various classes of working men and women; the Union Chargeability Act of 1865 allowing greater mobility of labour; the Labour Representation League of 1869, promoting working class members of parliament; and the Education Act of 1870 which sought to extend the educational franchise to the lower classes (Wigglesworth 1996, Taylor 2008). One of the major outcomes to arise during this period of policy generation was the generic increase of income for many workers. According to Vamplew (1988) wages rose sixty per cent between 1870 and the mid-1890s, and thus, over a period of approximately twenty years, the trade union movement had considerably improved pay scales and conditions for workers. More significantly for the invention of sporting tradition, trade union pressure had established a free Saturday afternoon (otherwise known as the Saturday half-holiday) for workers as a form of normal practice in many trades by the 1870s and this has been described by Brailsford (1991: 22) as '… the greatest revolution in the leisure calendar since the loss of Sunday'. Consequently those substantial changes to the working environment were the catalyst from which the leisure industry would grow and flourish (Cunningham 1980).

As a result of changes in work policy, men and women would acquire more resources (for example, disposable income and free time) than ever before. When combined, these conditions slowly set in motion increased demand for leisure activities and consequently, the circumstances needed to create a consumer market were beginning to take shape. To illustrate this point, note the following extract from a letter that was sent to and published by the editor of *The Times* newspaper on 11 November 1892.[3] In the letter, Mr James C. Marshall underscores the impact that the Saturday half-holiday has had on the development of leisure in Britain. He writes:

> The wide adoption of the Saturday half-holiday ... is an event of national importance ... This has undoubtedly tended to improve the physique of many thousands of employees of both sexes ... Numberless boating, cricket, football and tennis clubs, and many volunteer corps attest the wholesome use made of leisure now secured.

Thus, by the late nineteenth century mass sporting activities were seen to benefit directly from structural changes to the working environment. Sports participation had become fashionable and in vogue in the sense that associated activities were encouraged or popularised by rational re-creationists, who sought to introduce controlled leisure pursuits for the working man and woman (Holt 1990). The underpinning idea of this social movement was to produce and encourage participation in functional activities that were beneficial to the new industrial society, whilst remaining far removed from those unruly mob activities of the eighteenth century (Cunningham 1980, Elias and Dunning 1986). During this period of industrial rationalisation (Bauman 2000), sport and leisure too became rationalised and laced with qualities that were desirable and reflective of the period. For instance, Morgan (1994) writes of those conceptual similarities between new sports of the nineteenth century and the implemented values that were vital for the upkeep of the capitalist labour process. Equally, Guttman (1979) and Stewart (1989) describe how work-related techniques such as Taylorist and Fordist models were soon to be embedded within modern sport. This notion is further promoted by Calhoun (1987: 258) when he explains that new moral standards of the period such as 'self-government, respect for law, social service and good citizenship' were also ingrained within sporting activities. Consequently sports such as Association Football were promoted as dual functioning activities,

---

3 Marshall, J. 1892. 'Saturday Half-Holiday (A letter to the editor)' *The Times*, November 11: 14.

given their capacity to morally educate as well as entertain. On this logic, football was actively promoted and endorsed as a worthy pastime which could be easily distinguishable from earlier mob versions. Indeed, reminiscing on the evolution of football and its subsequent rise to an acceptable form of rational recreation, a correspondent for *The Times* newspaper (1887[4]) writes:

> In its origin it was distinctly plebeian. It was the game of the prentice lads of our big towns, who turned out en-masse on Shrove Tuesday and other public holidays and found in football a pleasurable diversion from the pastime of cracking heads … the modern game is at once inexpensive, healthy, manly, and exciting which unloosens for an hour or so the straight swaddling bands of civilised society, and, if properly played, teaches us discipline and chivalry.

The positive emphasis placed on football's manly qualities leads at once to its infusion with Muscular Christian values and this further illustrates the origins of the game within the British education system – and the continued influence of the Church more specifically (Dunning and Sheard 1979, Mason 1980, Mangan 1981, Taylor 1992, Dunning and Curry 2004). As a universal establishment, the Church had a role to play in the diffusion of the game from the public school elite into a mass cultural phenomenon. For instance, teams such as Aston Villa, Bolton Wanderers, Wolverhampton Wanderers and Everton were originally associated with religious organisations (Cunningham 1980: 127). Furthermore, Holt (1990) points out that in Birmingham (between 1870 and 1885) one in four football clubs were connected to religious organisations. Hence, with the vital support of the Church secured, football would reach and spread into all facets of social life – with teams representing old boys; teaching associations; church groups; places of work and the geographical regions/towns within which those teams were established.

Emerging Cultures: Experiential Consumption and Emotional Ties

Football was rapidly embraced by the mass population of nineteenth century Britain and consequently local teams became emblematic of something more than the activity (Huggins 1989). They were fast becoming an important feature of local culture (Tomlinson 1993) with team and supporter identities constructed to reflect the character and the imagined communities of their founding locality (Williams 1997, Croll 2000, Beaven 2005, Taylor 2008). This was often displayed and communicated through club symbolism such as club nicknames; badges; songs and ground locations (Brown 2008) that were used to

---

4 A correspondent. 1887. 'Football (Sport)'. *The Times*. March 18: 13

evoke a sense of passion and group unity within the lives of football supporters. Take the following from *The Times* newspaper (1893[5]) as an example of the impact that modern football had on the everyday lives of supporters:

> ... spectators of these league football matches are ... hot blooded ... and impulsive too. If the team of their town wins, well and good. Both the team and the directors (honest tradesmen these, for the most part) come in for applause and regard. A succession of disasters is, however, a dire calamity to the district. It means the diminution of self-respect to thousands.

In the same way that the urbanisation movement associated with mass industrial society and those concomitant government statutes for workers' rights made possible the audience for spectator football, it is also true that football gave rise to those circumstances through which new communities could gather together in shared time and space (Briggs 1968, Vamplew 1988). Others, too, highlight the importance of football for enhancing the collective experience and offering stability in a rapidly changing environment (Mason 1980, Holt 1990, Bale 1993, Tomlinson 1993); a situation that would also contribute to the onset of sporting rivalries amongst nineteenth century fans.

> ... fascination grips long after manhood is reached. Huge crowds of spectators collect and the keen rivalry between clubs, counties and countries have all grown up in the last two or three decades. (*The Times* 1887)[6]

Rivalries were quickly established between football teams based on geographical proximity and for those matches indicative of local rivalry, crowd expectancy would increase dramatically. For instance, Fishwick (1989: 52) indicates that local derbies between 'Wednesday' and 'United' in Sheffield would double the average gate. He states 'these were occasions when every Sheffielder would wish to show his or her allegiance to one or other of the major clubs'. Rippon (1981: 52) reports similar events occurring in the first Tyne and Wear derby between Sunderland AFC and Newcastle United, when '30,000 supporters attended this match on Christmas Eve 1898'. The average attendance for Sunderland matches in the same season was '12,300' (Tabner 2002: 96). So, as matches played on public holidays were likely to attract a larger audience, they often coincided with derby matches to add to the attractiveness (Fishwick 1989) and thus, the commercial potential of spectator football was acknowledged.

5　A correspondent. 1893. 'Professional Football (Sport)'. *The Times*. September 25: 5.
6　A Correspondent. 1887. 'Football (Sport)'.*The Times*. March 18: 13.

Early Fandom as Consumption? Professionalism, Spectatorism and the Nascent Consumer Market.

Aligned with the emergence of spectator football Lewis (1997: 24) suggests that professionalism was often encouraged and instigated from approximately 1885 onwards. He states that this was 'prompted by local rivalries ... to sign better players' and to attract a wider fan base – with others supporting this suggestion (Mason 1980, Arnold 1989, Walvin 1994, Russell 1997). Similarly, according to Symanski and Kuypers (1999: 4), the beginnings of commercialisation and professionalism were 'two sides of the same coin', given that the best players attracted the biggest crowd, and gate money paid for the best players. Tischler (1981) adds to this when he argues that football clubs could not afford to be complacent on this issue. He states: 'the entrepreneur could not assume that his customers would continue to contribute to the gate if the team lost – or the quality of the play was poor.' As a consequence, he explains that those clubs that had embraced the commercial potential of football began to apply pressure on the Football Association (FA) in a galvanised movement to legalise professionalism. This was achieved in 1885 following well-documented struggles (see Vamplew 1988: 51-73; Wigglesworth 1996: 45-61).

Whilst the FA had been in existence since 1863 and was initially formed by a small number of amateur clubs that were situated in Southern England; the Football League (established in 1888), by comparison, was distinctly Northern and professional in composition (Mason 1980, Benson 1994, Walvin 1994). It was clear from the outset that the Football League would support a professional philosophy and this included commercial logic in the sense that 'audience' and 'demand' were substantial considerations for professional football clubs (Wigglesworth 1996: 35). All of the member clubs at the inauguration of the Football League were from the Northern half of England and were established in sizable industrial locations that enjoyed a large and popular following.[7] By 1911, 34 out of the 36 towns with a population over 100,000 people had professional football teams, many of which had already attained the status of 'substantial businesses' (Wigglesworth 1996: 54). As evidence of this, Wigglesworth cites the example of Tottenham Hotspur Football and Athletic Company (established in 1899), a club that had secured gate receipts in excess of £6,399 in 1915 and by 1933 it returned a profit of £8,954 from receipts totaling £52,192. It should be noted, however, that profit on this scale was not for the sole benefit of club directors and chairmen due to restrictions put in place by the FA. In 1889, for

---

7 The twelve founding teams in the English Football League were: Aston Villa, Accrington Stanley, Blackburn Rovers, Bolton Wanderers, Burnley, Derby County, Everton, Nottingham County, Preston North End, Stoke City, West Bromwich Albion and Wolverhampton Wanderers.

instance, the FA placed a 'limit of five per-cent of the paid up shared capital' as the maximum dividend that a member club could pay out (Holt 1989: 283). This was raised to seven and a half per cent in 1920, to ten per cent in 1974, and fifteen per cent in 1983 (Szymanski and Kuypers 1999: 16). On such grounds, authors, such as Sloane (1971) and Holt (1989) reject the idea that football clubs were pure profit maximisers; however, maximising income did become critical for maintaining the club financially and this lead to the introduction of established business methods into the operations of football clubs. Szymanski and Kuypers (1999: 7) explain:

> ... the basic elements of football business ... have been [present] since the earliest days of the professional game: A product (entertainment of the game) supplied by workers (players and coaching staff) using land (grounds), buildings (stadiums) and equipment (ball, boots, kit) for a wage and sold to customers (supporters and other spectators) in competition and through co-operation with rivals.

The element of co-operation cited above, refers specifically to the business cartel strategy of the Football League (Fort and Quirk 1995). In order that its members were protected, rules were imposed to control competition for fans by fixing minimum ticket prices so that no club could undercut another (Tischler 1981). Likewise, competition for players was controlled by a retain and transfer system that worked in favour of the holding club, and to the detriment of the player (Taylor 2008, Goldblatt 2010); though it is plausible to suggest that the maximum wage may have been breached with regularity via the ingenuity of club directors who did not want to broadcast the systematic evasion of FA rules (Holt 1989). Furthermore, as Tischler (1981: 69) argues, football resembled a microcosm of the larger business environment, dealing in sports in the same way that others traded in houses, food and pencils. 'The natural order of the workplace', he insists, 'found its extension in football'.

Notwithstanding the business frame applied to the running of football clubs, it became clear that working people would willingly devote a relatively high proportion of their sport related expenditure, to watching rather than playing (Taylor 2008). It is suggested that football's popularity was positively reinforced by communication technologies such as printing, the media and rising levels of literacy within the British population more generally (Wigglesworth 1996). Publications such as *The Sporting Life* (1859), *Athletic News* (1875) and more specifically the rise of the Saturday night *Sports Special* (newspaper) cemented this relationship with the British public, uncovering the commercial demand for football and its place within British culture. Richard Holt (1990: 307) maintains that sport and newsprint '... became as much a part of the cultural scene as the gas lamp and the fish and chip shop ...' with spectator sport becoming part of a wider system of entertainment. Other technological advancements such as the nationwide introduction of the railway system have also contributed to this movement by making travel accessible and relatively inexpensive for spectators and for tourism more generally. By the late 1920s 'football special' trains were a common occurrence, as supporters began to travel in order to watch their teams away from home, especially in cup competitions:

> In all 83 cup-tie specials carrying 40,000 football fans will be run by the London Midland and Scottish. Birmingham is sending eight train loads and Manchester and Liverpool, five each. Bolton supporters have chartered six special trains. (*The Manchester Guardian* 1926)[8]

Consequently, within a relatively short space of time, League games and the Football Association Cup competition (FA Cup) attracted large travelling audiences. According to Hargreaves (1986: 66) the average attendance at the FA Cup final between 1893 and 1903 was 80,000, 'until 1913, when 120,000 *paying customers* jammed Crystal Palace Stadium to capacity'. Of this experience, a contemporary correspondent wrote:

> The largest crowd ever seen at a football match in England gathered on the Crystal Palace ground on Saturday afternoon to see, or at any rate hear, Aston Villa beat Sunderland one goal to nothing in the Association Football Cup competition. The number of spectators entering the ground was 121,919, which easily beats the "record" of 110,000 set up twelve years ago when Tottenham Hotspur drew with Sheffield United. (*The Times* 1913)[9]

Journalistic accounts like this one are useful in the sense that they offer valuable information regarding the experiences that were likely to be endured by the travelling football crowd. For example, reports of crowd composition, representation and expenditure were noted by the correspondent:

> The number of *excursionists* arriving at the terminal stations had certainly never been equalled … and from all one heard and saw they had more money to spend than on any former visit to London … Since nearly everybody was wearing either the Aston Villa or the Sunderland colours it would seem to follow that the proportion of invaders from the Midlands and the North was larger than usual. (*The Times* 1913)

---

8 A correspondent. 1926. 'Cup final trains'. *The Manchester Guardian*, April 26: 11.

9 A correspondent. 1913. 'Sporting Intelligence. The Football Association Cup: The crowd at the Crystal Palace'. *The Times*. April 21: 121.

Within this account, clear reference is made to the spending power of travelling fans, termed 'excursionists' in the sense that they had travelled by train to spend money outside of their local economy. Moreover, amidst the popularity of football and the clear commercial potential associated with mass support, it was also apparent that facilities were not yet geared up to cater for mass football crowds:

> Probably a third of those who pay to see these matches hardly got to see a glimpse of the play, and those that did see it, saw it under conditions that were depressingly uncomfortable … The bulk of spectators were situated on the sloping banks on the Southern side of the ground, and these, softened by the recent heavy rains, soon became mud slides on which the swaying multitude found it difficult to keep their feet. It is the duty of Football Association officials … to improve the layout of the cheaper proportions of the ground … The Ibrox Park disaster[10] was a warning that all possible precautions should be taken. (*The Times* 1913)

The stadia experiences of travelling football supporters (described here as 'depressingly uncomfortable') suggest that safety and comfort did not feature predominately on the agenda of event organisers, and this, according to Taylor (1992: 11) was not uncommon. He points out '… often the first improvements at football grounds were simply attempts to make sure that spectators paid to watch'. With this, turnstiles; fencing; the construction of primitive stands; 'earth mounds and wagons for spectators to stand on' were all designed to control the movement of the crowd and 'to ensure that they paid for the privilege' (Mason 1980: 140). Thus, as soon as football became a form of mass entertainment, facilities were required for supporters, and in turn those facilities demanded expenditure which had to be covered by entrance charges. In this capacity football was a business with entrepreneurs responding to the economic stimuli underpinning the growth of nineteenth century commercialised leisure (Szymanski and Kuypers 1999, Taylor 2008, Vamplew 1988).

Entrepreneurs would take many forms and could include the most unusual suspects. Local farmers, for instance, were known to capitalise on the local football match. Taylor (1992: 11) notes that 'if hills overlooked the pitch', as they did at the cup replay between Bolton and Notts County in 1884, 'four or five thousand supporters might gather in the farmers field … though the farmer charged half price for admission'. Less surprisingly, industrialists too began to cater for the football audience. Walvin (1994: 64-6) notes that from

---

10 This is a reference to the Ibrox Park disaster of 1902, when at an international match between England and Scotland, a wooden 'upper tier' stand collapsed under the weight of supporters and 25 people died.

the 1880s, football merchandise was produced by (for example) Lewis's of Manchester – offering for sale 'knickerbockers'[11] at 6s 9d (approximately 34 pence); 'jerseys' for 3s 11d (approximately 20 pence); and hand sewn footballs for 10s 6d (approximately 53 pence). He notes that even 'manufacturers of herbal and patient medicines directed their attention to thousands of players whose knocks, bruises and strains required swift, cheap and uncomplicated treatment'. Elliman's Embrocation was commercially known as 'the lubricant of football success'; Grant's Morell Cherry Brandy – 'the best tonic for football players and spectators on a winter's afternoon' and even a design of specialised footwear (football boots) – were made on mass as manufacturers considered it worthwhile to diversify into football specialisms, given the growing economic importance of the game:

> Even seed merchants supplied the new demand for durable turf ... Department stores offered the whole range of football goods, from nets to balls. In fact the economic spin-off from the game had, within thirty years of the establishment of the FA, become a sizable industry itself, and around football there have developed a cocoon ancillary trades and services all of which were made possible by the increasing amount of money made available for leisure. (Walvin 1994: 66)

It is clear, then, that catering for large urban populations of football fans could be reasonably lucrative, not only for football clubs (which were fast becoming private limited companies[12]) but also for train companies; the media and manufacturers of football merchandise in the form of playing equipment; medicines; umbrellas; streamers; rattles; scarves and beer (Benson 1994). On the latter point, publicans were quick to associate themselves with football and in some cases they were integral to the organisation of the game for both fans and football clubs alike (Vamplew 1988). As football clubs were set up and large crowds assembled to watch matches, publicans responded in varying ways. Mason (1980: 27) points out that in order to associate themselves with the local football club (for reasons of commercial gain) publicans would rent out grounds as changing rooms. He explains that in the early years 'there would be few other places in towns or villages which would be able to let out rooms in which a football team could change or hold meetings'. However, football clubs were anything but passive in negotiations for services, often playing the local market in order to strike the best deal or to argue for the improvement of facilities:

---

11 Knickerbockers are mens' or boys' knee length trousers. They were particularly popular in the early twentieth century when they were used and marketed as sports clothing.

12 According to Taylor (1992: 12) the transformation of football clubs into private limited companies worked to seal off the original supporters from any significant involvement in the club affairs.

Sunderland, for example, played their first matches on the field next to the Blue House Inn but found the £10 annual rent too much so moved to a site at Ashbrooke. Everton, despite being deeply indebted to the brewer John Houlding and playing on the fields adjoining his Sandon Hotel, quarrelled with him over rental charges, which led to him and founding Liverpool FC. Wolves and Arsenal both clashed with their publican landlords and moved grounds. (Collins and Vamplew 2000: 7)

As well as those pubs directly involved in the origins of football clubs, many others benefited from mass custom. The directors of Mitchells and Butlers, for instance, commissioned a study in 1910 which revealed that pubs near the Hawthorns (West Bromwich Albion's ground) showed increased takings on the Saturday of home matches. Moreover, local public houses became key outlets for the sale of Saturday night Sport Specials, which themselves were filled with advertisements by publicans (Collins and Vamplew 2000: 7). So with clear opportunities for money to be made, the evolution of spectator football was such that by the early decades of the twentieth century, its importance had grown to the extent that it was considered to be a dominant aspect of leisure. In the 1908/09 season six million people watched First Division matches, producing an average crowd per match of about sixteen thousand yet, by the 1937/38 season the comparable figures were approximately fourteen million and thirty thousand (Jones 1986: 38). Additionally, successful players and clubs began to profit from advertising and this, in turn, helped to expand the commercial potential of football in this period (Holt 1989). The weekly football results too, were vital to the gambling industry and in the 1930s, via the 'Football Pools' alone, between ten and fifteen million people per week were 'sending off postal orders totalling £800,000 to the Football Pools company' (Clarke and Critcher 1985: 75). It is important to note however, that 'Pools' success occurred despite the anti-gambling stance of the Football League and the Ready Money Football Betting Act 1920, which sought to prohibit all forms of gambling on football. Even when the Pools company found a loophole in this clause, the Football League reclaimed power by withholding the announcement of fixtures until two days before they were due to be played. Yet, under pressure from the press and the clubs that were losing money, 'the Football League backed down and accepted a cut of the money' (Goldblatt 2010: 185).

In spite of the early popularity and commercial potential of football, levels of support could not be guaranteed in light of a growing leisure market that would offer new and novel ways for working men and women to spend their leisure time. Cinema; music and dance; radio and even the annual holiday became competition for football's mass audiences. By 1926 there were over three thousand cinemas in the UK 'with a cumulative weekly attendance of twenty million' (Clarke and Critcher 1985: 71) and in 1936 the total gross box office receipts were 'approximately forty-one million pounds' (Rowson 1934: 37). In addition, the number of wireless licenses increased from '2,178,259 in 1926 to 9,082,666 in 1938' (Jones 1986: 37) bringing a new form of leisure into the home. Furthermore, by the 1960s television technology had become affordable for many homes throughout Britain, with BBC and ITV channels in full operation by the mid-1950s (Horrie 2002; Horne 2006). Thus, in order to survive, grow and remain financially viable, football required the implementation of a serious commercial strategy.

English Football Fandom in the Latter Twentieth Century: Demise and Redemption

King's (1997) historical analysis of the football industry post-1940 reveals that towards the latter period of the twentieth century, the steady decline of industry was matched with falling attendances and lack of investment in English football. King argues that the gradual move to a post-Fordist leisure centred state was further propelled by the newly elected Conservative government established in the late 1970s and he notes that these political changes had revolutionary consequences for the English game. To further contextualise matters it is important to note that football had become notorious as a problematic pastime due to its association with football hooliganism, an issue that was prevalent throughout the 1960s–1980s (see Taylor 1971a, 1971b, Clarke 1978, Dunning, Murphy and Williams 1988, Armstrong and Harris 1991, Armstrong 1998, Dunning, Murphy and Waddington 2002, Gibbons, Dixon and Braye 2008). Thus, with a tarnished reputation for spectator violence, football fandom was sitting uncomfortably as an activity that was, for all intents and purposes, digressing rather than progressing in line with the leisure revolution that was occurring elsewhere. For example, journalist Richard Rider (*The Times* 1982[13]) explains the position of spectator football in relation to 'new' emerging consumer activities. He writes:

> The reality is that spectators … do not visit football grounds as pilgrims rediscovering their roots and reliving the discomfort tolerated by their fathers. Thirty years ago, Saturday afternoon entertainment was limited. Now the motor car, television, and a whole host of alternative leisure activities offer a wider range of choice. While cinemas, pubs and other places of entertainment have had to modernise their facilities to meet the expanding and more discerning demands of the consumer, football grounds remain as relics of the pre-war

---

13 Rider, R. 1982. 'Why soccer is into injury time'. *The Times* August 8: 8.

period. Who at the age of thirty, longs to stand on a windy terrace, watching two mediocre teams when warmth and television beckon?

Whilst the status of the consumer was raised in the majority of social spheres as a reaction to neo-liberal policy, football had failed to embrace change in the same way. Spectators were herded through turnstiles, caged into stadiums, and rather than enhancing the experience for fans, directors and chairmen of football clubs were more concerned with the restraining features of the football ground in terms of crowd control. As Goldblatt (2010: 184) confirms, football was a business, 'but a very conservative and unusual business'. It was a 'low risk, low investment, low return game that distrusted innovation and ignored the competition from other sports' – such as basketball and ice hockey which found space amongst inner city redevelopments and deindustrialisation (Crawford 2004). Competition was also derived from a wider competitive, consumer-based leisure industry that offered opportunities to buy attractive experiences such as ice skating; skiing; outdoor pursuits; health spas; tanning salons; luxury gymnasiums; and computer gaming – to name only a few examples (Brown, Crabbe and Mellor 2008). In comparison to such activities, football terraces were unattractive, outdated and in need of refurbishment. Perhaps it is unsurprising to note, then, that aggregates of football crowds began to suffer. For instance Guttmann (1986) points out that crowds for First Division football matches in 1940s England averaged 41,000 and three decades later they averaged only twelve thousand. Amongst other possible causes, lack of customer services was listed as a potential contributory factor towards this trend (Smith and Stewart 2007). Negligence and ill treatment of fans was most poignantly demonstrated through the football disasters of 1985 and 1989[14] resulting in two major government inquiries. The Popplewell report of 1985 and the Taylor report of 1989 sought to discuss issues of safety, crowd control and the subsequent financial investment that would be needed to realise the long term sustainability and growth of the English football industry. Amidst concerns for safety and the legal obligation for clubs in the top two tiers of English football to change previously standing-room-only terraces to all-seated stadia, fans were centralised in a conscious attempt to rebrand football as a safe, enjoyable leisure pursuit and viable business.

Perhaps two of the most influential factors that would shape the future direction of football as a spectator sport were the initiation of the English

---

14 Following both the fire at Bradford and the physical unrest at Heysel, there was another disaster at Sheffield Wednesday's 'Hillsbrough' stadium. In 1989 Hillsbrough stadium was to host an FA Cup semi-final match between Nottingham Forest FC and Liverpool FC. The match was abandoned in the early moments of the game as excessive overcrowding within one of the stands eventually led to 96 fatalities.

Premier League (which would have commercial independence from the FA) and its associated contract with satellite television network BSkyB. The Premier League was formed in 1992 when teams in the then 'First Division' broke away from the rest of the Football League in order to ensure that England's most successful teams would retain most of their television revenue. Prior to this, the money that was paid by television was shared between all league clubs 'regardless of whether they had appeared on television that season' (Boyle and Haynes 2004: 21). Moreover, added competition from global broadcasters to screen English football introduced a largely domestic English football industry to the rigours of the world market. Thus, since 1992 BSkyB have secured exclusive rights to televise a proportion of FA Premier League matches, and in turn those matches are sold to customers on a subscription and/or pay-per-view basis.[15]

Notwithstanding the fact that satellite television was the catalyst that injected finance into the top tier of English football and thus stimulated the market, football clubs and other capitalist organisations also began to exploit new areas of consumer spending on an unprecedented scale. So, whilst it is plausible to suggest that a small proportion of football merchandise may have been sold to fans since the early part of the twentieth century, it was clear that by the century's end football-related merchandise was present everywhere – as journalist S. Winterburn (*The Guardian* 1998[16]) describes:

> … Christmas, a special time to gather among the Arsenal quilt sets and the Liverpool soap on a rope … Someone somewhere might be generous enough to present you with a £179.99 Chelsea mobile phone, available in both home and away colours as is Blackpool's more realistically priced mug. At £2.95 each … they can afford to keep one at home and take another on their travels … Before they have even grown out of their nappies they have already been targeted as potential spenders. The tiny Barnsley fan can opt for a suit bearing "I'm a little Tyke" message for just £15.99, or a baby grow for £8.99. For those who have outgrown romper suits … you may opt for the rather more subtle framed picture … The Manchester United fan is well accommodated for with a signed print of the 1968 European Cup reunion, retailing at £270.

In order for the scope and depth of merchandising (above) to become a reality, football clubs initiated marketing, sales and customer service departments to dream up new and innovative ways to sell merchandise and new experiences

---

15 For a thorough analysis of this transitional period for television and sport see Boyle and Haynes (2004: 7-45) *Football in the New Media Age*; Boyle and Haynes (2000: 22-45) *Power Play: Sport, the Media and Popular Culture*.

16 Winterburn, S. 1998 'Geared up for a festive season'. *The Guardian*, December 19: 11.

to earnest football fans. This, according to some, has had an obvious and irreversible effect on football culture. Like others, columnist Julie Welsh (*The Guardian* 1998[17]) reminisces about a forgotten past where 'football clubs were found in convenient, mid-town locations with a modest office at the front and a forecourt full of awestruck kids bunking off school to catch a glimpse of their heroes'. She argues that such scenes are now extinct and are reduced to memories for those lucky enough to have experienced this before football clubs were slowly motivated by the pursuit of money and consequently, the argument for this chapter has turned full circle. As I have explained throughout the course of this chapter, there is nothing new or paradoxically 'newsworthy' regarding the presence of consumption within the realm of football fandom. I have already pointed to evidence which suggests that from the latter part of the nineteenth century: (a) local derby matches were played on public holidays to ensure maximum gate receipts (Fishwick 1989); (b) professionalism was prompted by local rivalries and to stimulate the fan base (Lewis 1997); (c) by 1915 some football clubs were returning substantial profits from gate receipts (Wigglesworth 1996); (d) spectators were travelling to away matches on soccer special train services in the early twentieth century (Hargreaves 1986); and (e) pub landlords (Vamplew 1988), farmers (Taylor 1992), gambling institutions (Clarke and Critcher 1985), the media (Holt 1990) and other entrepreneurs have always found ways to profit by stimulating a desire for consumption acts.

Though commercial attitudes toward football and football fandom are nothing new, authors are right to point out that they have certainly intensified. The techniques used to exploit the market have advanced exponentially in late modern life, affording different and plentifully more consumption opportunities for fans to purchase or experience. However, the overt level of consumption in late modern life has led some to exaggerate anecdotal differences between fans of modernity (perceived traditional fans) and those of late modernity (consumers). Moreover, this rhetoric has grown to become commonplace, not only within the public domain (for example, through the media) but also within academic discourse, and this has important implications for the accurate theorisation of football fandom. In Chapter 3 I turn to address this concern when I argue that theoretical accounts of fandom practice (based on the logic noted above) are fundamentally flawed. Furthermore I contend that a new way of theorising is required in order to account for the complexity of football fandom cultures as they evolve with time.

---

17 Welsh, J. 1998 'Don't bother phoning the club unless you want a duvet cover', *The Guardian*, September 14: 7.

Chapter 3

Theorising Football Fandom as Consumption: Outlining the Need for an Alternative Approach

The 'cultural turn' raises interesting questions for critical traditions within the sociology of sport (Horne 2006: 1).

Within the sociology of sport, the historical shift from work- to leisure-centred capitalism that took place in England between the late nineteenth and early twentieth centuries has given rise to academic discussions regarding the cultural turn. Consequently, fresh debates about the relationship between new leisure activities and social structure have ensued (see quote above, Horne 2006). For instance, the cultural turn has encouraged theories which express the positive value that new consumption (associated with leisure) can offer in terms of emancipation, individuality, creativity and identity. Equally, however, those theories are countered by pessimistic interpretations suggesting that late capitalist society merely serves to veil an advanced form of capitalist oppression which serves to exploit new forms of mass leisure and consumption for its own ends (Bennett 2005). In this chapter I explain how such diverse theoretical positions have impacted on research into the phenomenon of football fandom and I further suggest that a new theoretical perspective is warranted to more accurately depict the nature of fandom in late modern life. In order to outline the need for an alternative theoretical approach I begin by highlighting the failure of previous dichotomies and typologies of football fandom before criticising more recent post-modern applications.

The Ultimate Failure of Football Fandom Dichotomies and Typologies

In some respects the sociology of sport seems to have become enclosed by those old paradigms that were once its new bold points of reference. (Blackshaw 2002: 200)

Early approaches to sport fandom have made attempts to account for the co-existence of solid-modern and late modern living. For instance, Clarke (1978) makes a conceptual distinction between 'genuine fans' (for example, those who identify heavily with a sense of community and tradition) and 'other types' of supporters (for example, those primarily interested in football as entertainment). This simple dichotomy has been used to explain how certain groups have been marginalised by the late modern onset of commercialisation in football. Moreover, it has been reiterated and repackaged by a number of academics since. For example, Boyle and Haynes (2000) distinguish between 'traditional' and 'modern' fans; Nash (2000a) between 'core' and 'corporate' and Quick (2000) between 'irrational' and 'rational' fans. Although the terminology used differs between authors, the overriding message is similar. New fans and traditional fans are often perceived as distinct from one another in terms of the means, motives and underlying philosophies that they hold. As Mehus (2010: 897) reports, 'good supporters are often contrasted with bad consumers'.

'New fans' (that is, bad consumers) are commonly conceived as affluent, distant, rational and even obscure individuals in the sense that solidarity, identity and adherence of support are held to question. More specifically, scholars Rein, Kotler and Shields (2006) imply that sports fans have never before had so much choice and opportunity to spend their time and money. Consequently, fans are accused of being 'elusive' in the sense that loyalty cannot be assumed due to heightened competition for consumer attention. For example, it has been noted that the proliferation of media channels dedicated to sports can offer even more convenient cost- and time-effective ways of remaining in touch with objects of fandom (Nash 2000b, Weed 2008) and in turn, this has led some scholars to suggest that fans are becoming less defined by 'traditional' social groupings. Instead, it is implied that fandom is now mediated by accelerated commodification processes, and consequently more opportunities exist for agents to 'do fandom alone – and from a distance' (Boyle and Haynes 2004: 139). On the contrary, 'traditional fans' are described as those with strong emotional connections, rooted together with group loyalties. As a consequence, they are portrayed as irrational and yet predictable beings in the sense that they blindly follow group conventions and as such, it is thought that they have the potential to be manipulated by corporate bodies.

When taken together these views assume a dichotomy between two distinct fractions of proposed fandom types and yet, such accounts are in danger of presuming rigid distinctions which mask the reality subsumed within the lived experience. Crawford (2004) for one concurs with this observation when he points out that much contemporary work seeks to establish the belief that – through rampant commercialisation – English sport is losing its inherently traditional qualities that were characteristic of a so-called past 'golden age'. The most alarming point for Crawford is the contribution that this line of thought has had towards, what he terms, 'the endless quest for fandom authenticity' within the sociology of sport (2004: 34). This quest, he argues, tends to over simplify the phenomenon under study via the creation of typologies or blind acceptance of fandom 'types'. For example, consider the work of social psychologists Wann, Melnick, Russell and Pease (2001) when they distinguish between the authenticity of 'traditional' sports fans when compared against 'sports spectators/consumers'. Similar to previous models, the latter group (consumers) are used by the authors to refer to individuals that are thought not to have the same degree of involvement with the object of fandom as the former category of traditional sports fans might. Furthermore Wann et al. extend this argument when they sub-divide sports consumers into two groups: 1. 'Direct' where sports consumption involves personal attendance at a sporting event and 2. 'Indirect' where consumption involves watching sport through the mass media or consuming sport via the Internet. Consequently, the authors consider fans as either 'Highly' or 'Lowly' identified with their team/club due to 'types' of consumption activities that they engage with or perform. Some, such as attending games in person, wearing team colours and actively yelling for a team, were viewed by the researchers as more authentic and thus, those activities were thought to signify a greater affiliation with sports teams or clubs than other activities or performances might.

In this sense, authenticity is often attributed to a romanticised vision of 'traditional' which is reportedly under attack from processes of globalisation, post-modernity and consumer culture more generally. Anthony King (1997; 1998) was perhaps the first scholar to actively seek empirical evidence for this when he paid specific attention to a group of fans (considered to be 'traditional') and monitored their thoughts and behaviours in light of the more recent transformations of football in England and the rise of the FA Premier League. King was ultimately interested in the discovery of how traditional fans position themselves in relation to the commodification of football and in light of what he conceives to be a new affluent or consumer audience. Using a Gramsci-inspired theoretical framework, he argues that intervention from above (that is, the neo-liberal endorsement of privatisation espoused by the 1980s Conservative Government) had impacted severely on traditional aspects of fandom culture, causing some elements of practice to change indefinitely. The results of King's ethnographic research uncovered a partial form of resistance by traditional fans (to consumerism in football) in the sense that they were shown to display discontent with changes to the game and yet they simultaneously displayed elements of acceptance. For example, the studied group were unhappy with changes to ticket pricing and yet they were willing to pay escalating fees. Concomitantly, while they were vocal about the demise of standing spaces which were central to their solidarity, they were proud of their modernised stadium and so forth. In conclusion King notes that the behaviours, conflicts, thoughts and aspirations of those within his sample could not be explained using a one dimensional argument of resistance to the bourgeoisification of football and therefore he asserts that a more sophisticated form of study and theorisation is required.

Two of the most prominent accounts of football fandom include Redhead's (1993) view of fans as either 'Participatory' or 'Passive' and Giulianotti's (2002) ideal-type taxonomy of football fans. First, Redhead highlights the conflicting nature of 'participatory' and 'passive' forms of football fandom. He suggests that one outcome derived from the rise of the service sector in England (and the expansion of white collar workers) was the emergence of a new type of 'active' supporter. The active supporter (for Redhead) is typified by, and can be evidenced through, the development and rise to popularity of fanzines and supporter organisations. Conversely, and perceived as an adversary to the active fan, Redhead argues that 'passive' supporters have also been growing in stature over the same period (1980–1990s). This, he notes, has occurred in response to the increasing number of consumer products (including television coverage) relating to the game and the allure of consumption for consumption sake. Thus, whilst scholars (for example, Cleland 2010) are right to point out that Redhead does not categorise fans within a simplistic dichotomy as such, the work reaches similar conclusions towards segmentation between perceived groups of fans.

Giulianotti's taxonomy of spectator identities in football presents a more comprehensive theoretical model, but again, its suitability for real life application is questionable. As with previous models, the author attempts to categorise various types of fans into distinct areas depending on the manner via which fandom is performed and ultimately consumed. For instance, he claims that certain characteristics of fan types can be identified along a horizontal axis from the 'Traditional' to the 'Consumer'. Adding to this familiar dichotomy Giulianotti places a vertical axis mid-way between these points, running between Hot to Cool forms of fandom. As such, this creates four quadrants into which spectators may be classified as 'more' to 'less' authentic (Supporter; Follower; Fan or *Flâneur*). Those quadrants identified (above) are based on the relationships with and proximity to football spaces (for example, club stadia and the local community); the means of consuming live football (for example, 'in person' versus 'via the media'); interactions with other fans (for example, 'face-to-face' versus using 'new media communications') and other aspects that are thought to depict levels of solidarity and identity around football practice. Collectively, those conditions are considered by the author to help determine how football fans are to be categorised in relation to authenticity. But whilst this typology is insightful enough to point out the vast and varied means via which fans can engage with the practice, ranking authenticity via perceived importance of consumption type can cause practical problems for transference into real situations. For example, Giulianotti's category of 'Cool/Consumer Spectators', reads as follows:

> The cool consumer spectator is a football *flâneur*. The *flâneur* acquires a postmodern spectator identity through a depersonalised set of market-dominated virtual relationships, particularly interactions with the cool media of television and the Internet. (Giulianotti 2002: 38)

Here for instance, Giulianotti makes a general assumption about the ways in which football fans use the Internet. Through classifying this mode of consumption with less interactive forms of media like television, Giulianotti suggests that the Internet is merely a virtual and passive form of communication that the inauthentic *flâneurs* use to experience football in a detached manner – instead of engaging in more real and authentic forms of fandom (for example, like attending matches in person and interacting face-to-face with other fans). Indeed, Giulianotti (2002: 39) argues that: 'the cool/consumer seeks relatively thin forms of social solidarity with other fellow fans', thus ignoring the vast number of what might be considered authentic football fans who, as well as attending games in person, also contribute to online discussion forums, blogs, email loops and message boards and use the Internet as just one form of communicating. In other words, the fluidity of fandom practice and significance of newer forms of consumption are missed in this conceptual taxonomy. Rather than viewing football fandom as a phenomenon that is constantly in flux, it holds onto dated assumptions of 'traditional' versus 'new' and champions a new, but principally deterministic, view of fandom types. Crawford (2004: 33) makes similar criticisms towards current theories of fandom. He writes:

> While it is possible to identify different levels of commitment and dedication to a sport and different patterns of behaviour of fans, it is important that we do not celebrate the activities of certain supporters and ignore (or even downgrade) the activities and interests of others ... Rather than privileging the activities of certain fans over others, it is important, if we are to understand the contemporary nature of fan cultures, that we consider the full range of patterns of behaviour of all fans, including those who do not conform to 'traditional' patterns or images of fan activities (Crawford 2004: 33)

To summarise, whilst many dichotomies and typologies of fandom have sought to explain fan behaviour in an all-encompassing manner, they spend too much time attempting to segregate and compartmentalise fandom types into idealistic but ultimately unrealistic components. Not only do some theoretical models of this nature lack empirical support to substantiate claims to practice, but they are theoretically rigid, inflexible and unyielding. Many models romanticise what are considered to be traditional forms of fandom and dismiss, downplay, or diminish the importance of evolving fandom activities. Yet, as King (1997) and Stone (2007) have previously brought to attention, perhaps fandom does not stand still long enough for traditional support to have ever really existed in the sense that it is portrayed. This has led current writings to explore post-modern explanations of contemporary football fandom practice.

Football Fandom and Post Modernity

In a growing segment of the current literature discussions of the 'post-fan' (a term first used by Redhead 1997) have begun to appear in opposition to typologies of fandom. For instance, Crabbe (2008) contends that scholars must take into account the changing nature of social life – with the blurring of previous boundaries, advancements of communications technology, new levels of consumption and ever more possibilities for individual choice. Rather than acknowledging disparate fractions of fandom types, Crabbe describes the emergence of a post-modern football community which differs radically from the traditional form that has so often featured at the centre of theoretical models. He asserts that football communities in the post-modern mould are less likely to be bound by colloquial closeness and are more likely to form what Blackshaw (2008a) terms 'deterritorised groupings' in the sense that they are short term; temporary and less intimate; characterised by intense emotional involvement; infrequent gatherings and rapid dispersals. Concomitantly, from this perspective football fans are said to 'perform' as opposed to 'live' group connections. Thus, individualism resides at the heart of such commentaries with fandom perceived as the performance of a self-gratifying function. Crabbe, in particularly, captures the professed sense of individuality in his anecdotal description of football fandom beyond the final whistle when he writes:

> ... individuals make their way home like disturbed rats scuttling for cover, eager to be ahead, separate from the crowd in a rush to get home. (Crabbe 2008: 435)

In a similar manner, Blackshaw (2008a) uses Bauman's (2000, 2001, 2005, 2007b) concept of 'liquid-modern' to suggest that solid structures of modernity have lost shape somewhat and have become liquefied and engulfed within consumer society. Thus, both Blackshaw and Bauman make clear the contemporary importance of consumption as an individualistic pursuit. For instance, Bauman writes:

> No lasting bonds emerge in the activity of consumption. Those bonds that manage to be tied in the act of consumption may, but may not, outlast the act; they may hold swarms together for the duration of their flight but they are admittedly occasion bound. (Bauman 2007a: 78)

Proponents of Bauman's work within the realm of sport sociology use similar analogies to suggest that swarms of sports fans gather in a multitude of places and spaces to consume football via the increasing proliferation of technological mediums. Kraszewski (2008) is one such scholar who refers to the liquid-modern conditions of relocation and displacement in association with sports fandom. He argues that the increasingly mobile United States (US) population use sport, and in particular American Sports Bars, to collect temporarily and connect with other fans who also find themselves displaced from their place of origin (that is, place of birth). Moreover, he asserts that through the consumption of sport, people turn to the idea of culture and community for a sense of comfort and self gratifying assurance. In this case, commercial American football bars are thought to fulfil an important role by providing places where displaced fans can meet for comfort, watch television, interact, offer temporary reassurance, or in other words, consume the false notion of community before returning to an individual existence. Blackshaw (2008a: 334) too concurs with this convenience use of the term 'community' in the sense that agents use it sparingly to suit individual circumstances. He writes:

> The modern fan only wants community the way that they want community, and that is individually wrapped and ready for consumption.

He contends that while liquid-moderns may like the sentiment of traditional community, they would be unwilling to make the sacrifices to personal freedom that would see them give up their individuality for the cause. Moreover and adding support for such speculation, Boyle and Haynes (2004) suggest that new football communities are now mediated by accelerated commodification which has sought to personalise fandom experiences. They assert that blogs, pod-casts and other social networking tools are growing in popularity and thus, choice and consumerism are key ingredients of contemporary football fandom. The most comprehensive empirical study offering a partial post-modern interpretation of football fandom stems from the work of Cornell Sandvoss (2003). Through an eclectic and interdisciplinary approach to the everyday football fan, spanning Bourdieu's (1984) analysis of consumption and taste, Ritzer's (1998) work on contemporary regimes of formal rationality and Baudrillard's (1983) vision of hyper-reality and simulation, Sandvoss argues that televised football and the increasing rationality of the modern game has led to a sense of contentlessness onto which fans can project themselves. He positions fans theoretically as post-modern citizens and borrows the term 'DIY citizenship' from Hartley (1999) to suggest that identity is chosen by individuals from a range of opportunities in the mediasphere and then communicated through acts of football consumption. Furthermore, given the standardization of contemporary football stadiums, Sandvoss argues (unlike Bale 1993) that fans are losing their connection to place; although I suggest that more research is required in order to substantiate this position. For example, the accusation that Sandvoss makes in relation to placelessness might hold true for fans of top tier clubs in their respective leagues (Chelsea, Bayer Leverkusen, DC United), however, it is yet unknown how far this can be projected onto the majority of fans associated with less successful or less globally appealing clubs. Consequently, I suggest that a greater body of evidence is required to substantiate or refute those claims made by Sandvoss and other post-modern theorists.

Theorising a Third Way for Football Fandom Studies

Academics have begun to question previous research in an attempt to rethink football fandom for the late modern period. John Williams (2007) for one, is critical of much of the literature in this domain. He criticises macro theories and simplistic dichotomies/typologies of fandom for romanticising the traditional and failing to position fans in the new social contexts of late modernity. Authors have, of course, addressed the latter using post-modern social critiques (Giulianotti 2002, Sandvoss 2003, Blackshaw 2008a, Crabbe 2008), however, they have been criticised by Williams for exaggerating the decline of traditional ties. Williams (2007: 142) suggests that there is 'a tendency for authors to oversimplify fandom' at either end of this theoretical continuum, based on normative speculation regarding new media-driven consumption patterns. He asserts that post-modern claims to practice may hold some validity but is also mindful that they require a combination of theory and rigorous empiricism to substantiate this position. Further, he argues that the search for explanations of rapid change often negate and underestimate the importance of continuity, place and community in English sport, especially football.

Gibbons and Dixon (2010) concur on this point. They suggest that the social and communal elements of football fandom have not disappeared in the manner that some have projected. In fact, rather than dissolving community, they argue that new lines of consumption (for example, new media communications) actually help to maintain it, albeit by non-traditional means. Thus, if fandom can be implicated within acts of consumption, then it is important to investigate the impact and significance of new modes of consumption practice (for example, such as Internet use) before reaching premature conclusions that devalue the significance of such actions. In sum, given that criticisms are cast on either side of the *macro* (structure) or *micro* (agency) spectrum, it is proposed that a *meso* (middle ground) approach would likely offer the most parsimonious solutions to current theoretical problems identified in this chapter. For example, while macro considerations suggest that social structures compel agents to engage in social manoeuvres and micro paradigms tend to assume that individuality is the root of all action, the meso level can provide a link between these dominant standpoints (Kirchberg 2007). Consequently, theoretical approaches that share a desire to understand how individual action is organised within mundane activities, whilst simultaneously recognising structural features that are reproduced through individual action, have much to offer in the current context.

Chapter Summary

Much of the recent work dedicated to the sociology of football operates at extreme ends of a theoretical dichotomy where fans are situated as either the product of macro level structures, or conversely, micro level, self-determining agents of post-modernity. In this chapter I have questioned the integrity of those perspectives and have argued that while each has merit, neither is sufficiently equipped to explain succinctly the complexities of football fandom practice in late modern life. In relation to those problems and without rejecting either perspective entirely, I have argued that football fandom research would benefit from an investigation of the theoretical space in between those accounts (for example, at the meso level) and this is congruent with recent calls to study the everyday experience of football fandom.

Chapter 4

Learning the Game: The Consumption of Knowledge and the Construction of 'Other' in Late Modern Fandom

In a game, the field (the pitch or board on which it is played, the rules, the outcomes at stake etc.) is clearly seen for what it is, an arbitrary social construct … By contrast, in the social fields, which are the products of a long, slow process of autonomisation, and are therefore, so to speak, games 'in themselves' and not 'for themselves', one does not embark on a game by a conscious act, one is born into the game, with the game; and the relation of investment, *illusio*, investment is made more total and unconditional by the fact that it is unaware of what it is. (Bourdieu 1990: 67)

I begin my primary analysis of football fandom as consumption with an exploration of the experiential processes involved with learning the game. Borrowing the following term from Bourdieu (see above quote, 1990) 'to play the game' one must know the game and knowing the game inevitably entails the genesis, acquisition and ultimate consumption of knowledge relating to various rules, genres, discourses and social norms that underpin any given practice. Those processes are, I suggest, a vital and yet under researched area of academic inquiry within the sociology of football and it is on this logic that I now turn to expose narrative accounts of fandom genesis that were offered by participants.

The most fundamental narrative offered in this sample involved the story of how participants became football fans in the first instance. In other words, participants documented their first experiences of practice and explained how those experiences had helped to develop future fandom behaviour. A common and predominant theme for many interviewees when discussing the genesis of their support was an explanation of the passing on or acquisition of knowledge – though subtle differences were reported as to how knowledge was acquired:

Bill: School was just all about football. PE and football practice was the only lessons we all looked forward to … Learning the craft was just a major part of the school experience. [Sunderland, aged 34 (MF)]

Paul: I think it was just your peers. Your mates. Football was the main diet … I used to go up 'the bob end[1]' at Ayresome Park … that's basically how I started to go to the ground. [Middlesbrough, aged 53 (STH)]

Louise: I've always been a football fan since I was younger cos my dad always supported Liverpool so I didn't have a choice in the matter because it's always surrounded me. My whole family are Liverpool fans, even my Nan. [Liverpool, aged 20 (MF)]

The examples cited above help us to visualise some of the various means through which social actors (for example, in this instance, children) begin to consume football. In the first extract (Bill) early recollections were often situated within institutions such as the schooling system, youth sports clubs and organisations such as 'the cubs' and 'scouts' where young children first begin to socialise with one another. Indeed all participants recalled early experiences of football in this type of environment where they claim to learn, or at least become socially aware of, the constitutive rules of the game. Notwithstanding the importance of the formalisation of sport's codifying rules, this was only one avenue through which the consumption of knowledge was derived. Participant Louise (above) provides an alternative and perhaps more familiar story of kinship coercion into the practice. She explains how fandom is almost hereditary in the sense that support for a particular football team can permeate generations of kin groups. Additionally, Paul (above) attributes fandom genesis to his friends and close peer groups and views football as the stabilising force that holds such friendships together. In what follows I take into account those fluid and variable explanations of fandom origins in order to emphasise the significance of such processes for theorising fandom cultures. Furthermore, I look beyond acquisition of the constitutive rules of the game (that are often developed through adult-organised competition) to expose the inner workings of those dominant themes of primary teaching (for example, kin or peer groups) that are fundamental to one's consumption of practice-specific knowledge.

Football Fandom Genesis and the Role of Peers

Keith: Cos, like, your mates. Everybody else was doing it at the time. My best mates were all football mad and I suppose it rubs off. [Middlesbrough, aged 45 (MF)]

---

1 The 'bob end' is an unofficial name (coined by football fans) given to a particular space within Ayresome Park Stadium (the previous home of Middlesbrough FC) where children would stand.

Watching professional football was understood as a shared experience and was described by many as a contagious mode of childhood consumption (often initiated between the ages of ten and sixteen years). Having already gained a general understanding of the practice before attending their first football match (discussed further 48-9) participants such as John (below) would hone their skills and knowledge, using various resources to engage with and act out the practice that they had observed from a distance in prior years:

John: My older brother had mates and they went to football but I was too young. I remember imagining what it would be like, I couldn't wait to be a part of it. So I used to knock about with some older lads, fetching the ball, just doing whatever I could to join in and then I'd go to watch the match with them. Then eventually everyone my age was going. All the lads from the estate, just playing football and going to the match together. [Middlesbrough, aged 42 (MF)]

When a practice is shared by a group of peers, researchers have argued that those people become a tool for inducting others into that group (Young 1988). Similarly, in relation to the genesis of football fandom, peers and siblings seemed to have a reciprocal effect, drawing one another into the practice. However, peer-inspired socialisation into the practice of football fandom was, for the most part, a gender-specific phenomenon. In this sense, female participants reported that 'feminine culture', or interactions between female peers, often excluded the concept of 'masculine' based activities such as football:

Kirsty: … As a kid I think you do what your friends do and unfortunately football was not a typical activity for girls. [Hartlepool, aged 33 (STH)]

Like Kirsty, Clair too acknowledges the point that football was perceived as a gender specific phenomenon.[2] She explains: 'because I played football with the lads from my street and supported my local football team I was looked down upon by loads of bitchy girls at school'. Thus, the barriers to participation for girls in this sample were more commonly associated with fellow female peers rather than male acquaintances. Clair confirms: 'I loved football, but they (female peers) all thought I was strange'. It appears then, that females within this sample were often more cautious in their outward expressions of football support and this had direct implications for self-perceptions of fandom (discussed later in this chapter: 62-4). For young males, however, geographical sociability was an essential aspect of fandom genesis and football offered a form of leisure consumption that was affordable, local and desirable. The desire to attend football matches was perhaps symptomatic of the overt encouragement that

2 Clair [Darlington, aged 36 (STH)].

male participants received from others to consume or participate as fans within the live venue. For instance, Tim (below) recalls how specific spaces within the football stadium were often unofficially allocated to them, given that they were, in his eyes, 'the future of football fandom':

> Tim: There was a group of us that went. We used to turn up at about three minutes to kick off and everyone like, left space for us. Even though there were no seats and we were just kids, the men always made space for us young'ns … That's how it should be. Everyone knows the importance of future fans. [Middlesbrough, aged 54 (MF)]

Specific locations such as the 'bob end' at Ayresome Park (previously noted by participant 'Paul') were thought by participants to serve a social function by ensuring a continuation of tradition, that is, continuously introducing the live venue to a new generation of young male consumers. Prior to the late 1980s, however, it is important to point out that spectator football was more accessible for children and many participants recalled experiences of gaining access to the stadium without any payment at all. This was due in part to stadium design, plus inadequate safety and security measures. Colin explains:

> Colin: At Ayresome Park we used to get what they called in them days a 'squeeze'. Basically someone lifts you over the turnstiles, so you don't exactly pay. So that money that you got off your parents you could spend on going to the baths [swimming pool], because in the 60s and 70s the prices for attendance were similar at both. Obviously that's not the case now, but it was then. [Middlesbrough, aged 53 (STH)]

With direct reference to ease of access and low admission fees, participants like Colin were only too aware that the conditions specific to their childhood experiences (for example, from the mid-late twentieth century) had altered significantly for the current generation of children. He spoke specifically about the introduction of season tickets as a means of stabilising gate receipts for the club and the associated effect that this is likely to have on the current youth.

> Colin: Obviously the price of tickets is a major issue but over the years, since it became all seater there is less chance for kids to get their own tickets. [Middlesbrough, aged 53 (STH)]

Notwithstanding fears for the future of football fandom, the experience of attending football matches with peers in late childhood was often synonymous with the first taste of parentally-blessed independence and a new-found freedom that young males were awarded through the consumption of football at the live venue:

> Bill: I mean it was one of the first big things that I was allowed to do totally independent of my parents. I lived a few miles away from Roker Park and often my parents were fairly strict about where I was allowed to go, but football was ok. They knew that I was going with stacks of mates and I suppose for lads it was expected. It was normal. [Sunderland, aged 34 (MF)]

To similar effect, participants like Jeff[3] also reinforce the point that going to the match was a *'rite of passage'* for young males. He elaborates: 'every lad I knew went to the match at some point when they were young' and with this, the 'ordinary' nature of fandom consumption for young males is noted. This assured reference given to the normality of football was also implicitly tied to concepts of masculinity. One's physical ability to play or, additionally, a substantial knowledge of the game, was seemingly traded amongst male youths for degrees of cultural acceptability:

> Dougie: I lived on a council estate in Sunderland where there were lots of other kids around and little scraps of land, and that's what you did. Same at school … Among my mates it was more important to be good at football than it was to be clever in lessons. Hundred percent fact! Being a hard lad or being good at football got you instant respect … Football was like a social badge for kids. Even if you were no good, you'd better show an interest in your team … For us it was screw education. It was just football, football, football! [Sunderland, aged 37 (STH)]

Dougie's account of this situation (above) can be partially explained with reference to Pierre Bourdieu's concept of 'cultural capital'. To make clear, Bourdieu (1984) uses this term to map relationships between class groups on the basis of dominance and subordination, and he does this on the relative amount of capital that each social group possesses. Accordingly, capital in multiple guises (for example, economic or cultural) often follows the privileged class, awarding a plethora of resources to be traded within one's culture. For instance, 'economic capital' (for example, accrued wealth) can be traded for an item or experience of monetary value, whilst 'cultural capital' (for example, a high level of education) can be traded for a desired job or social position. Bourdieu (1977: 187) explains:

---

3 Jeff [Newcastle, aged 27 (MF)].

Without entering into detailed analysis, it must suffice to point out that academic qualifications are to cultural capital what money is to economic capital.

In any instance, capital is thought to play a crucial role in the reproduction of dominant social relations and structures. This is particularly true with the ways in which certain forms of knowledge are unequally distributed and so knowledge, opportunity and consequently, 'capital', become markers of distinction and social privilege. However, in Dougie's situation (above) one distinct difference can be noted: Where Bourdieu subdivides dominant culture into a number of competing categories he does not allow that there are forms of cultural capital produced outside of and often against 'dominant' or 'official' modes. This is a point that other scholars reinforce when they call for an acknowledgment of two types of cultural capital, 'official' and 'popular' (Fiske 1992; Schatski 1997). As the situation applies to Dougie, the practice of football fandom offers a form of 'popular' cultural capital that is not typically dependent on, or convertible into, official capital in the Bourdieuian sense. Consequently, it is important to point out that popular cultural capital will not necessarily enhance one's career, nor will it produce or contribute to upward mobility in the sense that Bourdieu describes. Thus, the desirability of popular cultural capital within social practices like football fandom relates directly to the esteem that it creates amongst peers in a particular community of taste, rather than amongst social betters (Fiske 1992).

Communities of taste, like those mentioned above (for example, in this instance, centred on 'common culture' as oppose to 'high culture'), seem to stem from self-propagating histories of activities based on objective social conditions and accrued personal experiences. For Bourdieu (1984), this uncovers the important truth that inclination reflects social circumstance and he clarifies this via his most frequently used concept 'habitus':

> The structures constitutive of a particular type of environment ... produce the *habitus,* systems of durable dispositions, structured structures predisposed to function as structuring structures, that is as the principle of generation and structuration of practices and representations which can be objectively 'regulated' and 'regular' without in any way being the product of obedience to rules, objectively adapted to their goal without presupposing the unconscious orientation towards ends and the express mastery of the operations necessary to attain them and, being that, collectively orchestrated without being the product of the organizing action of a conductor (Bourdieu 1977: 72).

In this rather complex account, Bourdieu explains how seemingly spontaneous individual actions actually meet wider societal expectations and thus, he makes clear that individual dispositions inevitably hold cultural characteristics

(Wacquant 2008). Thus, habitus is used by Bourdieu to express the way in which individuals become themselves 'by developing attitudes and dispositions that are influenced by history, traditions and cultures operating within and between specific fields' (Bourdieu 1990: 54). Consequently, habitus directly influences practice and also determines an agent's response to different situations. Furthermore, as Bourdieu uses this concept, habitus is not simply responsible for action but also for thought, understanding, motivation and perceptions as well (Schatzki 1997). It is important to note that Bourdieu does not suggest that the action of the habitus is to determine fixed responses in practice. Rather, it limits the options that individuals have by providing cultural norms and historical precedents which in turn determine strategies of action or practice (Crawshaw and Bunton 2009).

In the current context, this is evident within Dougie's attitude towards education. His enthusiasm for football and contempt for school work is symptomatic of a wider habitus, through which capital is decided by non-official routes. These findings bear similarities to the work of Paul Willis (1979) when he describes a process where working-class children develop a resistance to the education system, often emphasising its irrelevance to their future employment prospects. This process, he claims, can explain how working-class children end up in working-class jobs and he refers to this reality as a form of counter-culture that is bound up, more generally, within a larger working-class identity – given that agents are heavily influenced by their social background (for example, objective structural conditions) and the practices that they are engaged with at an everyday level. He writes:

> The introduction posed the question of how and why it is that working class lads come to accept working class jobs through their own apparent choice. We can say that for a good proportion ... this is in the form of a *partial cultural penetration* of their own real conditions and a mystified celebration of manual work which nevertheless preserves something of a collective, rational, though incomplete, logic. I have suggested that this can be understood as a form of cultural reproduction which helps to contribute towards social reproduction in general (Willis 1979: 185)

With this in mind, further parallels can be made with the current data set in the sense that discussions of 'class' were implicated in participant responses and elements of cultural penetration and social reproduction were implied. The following accounts provided by self-proclaimed working-class and middle-class fans, respectively, typify those discussions:

Graham: It's a working class game man! Traditionally most good players come from working class backgrounds don't they?.. I remember comparing GCSE grades with people from the posh schools and they all had 'A' stars and what have you, but as far as we were concerned they were all faggots [laughing], you know, had no interest in football and they certainly couldn't play. It doesn't mean as much to them I don't think. [Newcastle, aged 43: Self-proclaimed working class childhood (STH)]

Michael: Well I don't mind saying that I went to a good school within the area but contrary to what people think, football was still a major talking point ... Sure, grades were the most important aspect of school but football was a close second ... I know it's a common stereotype that football's a working class game, but it's not if you think about it realistically for even a split-second. [Sunderland, aged 20: Self-proclaimed middle class childhood (MF)]

It is important not to misrepresent the frequency of, and the emphasis placed by participants on, 'class identity'. However, when this issue did emerge (for example, without promptings of the interviewer) it was predominately referenced by self-proclaimed working-class participants declaring authenticity or ownership over the game based on misplaced notions of historical reference, tradition or perceived commitment to the practice. Moreover, despite the fact that self-proclaimed middle-class participants set out to accumulate what Fiske (1992) would conceive as 'official' cultural capital through the achievement of successful school grades, they too worked (albeit as a secondary feature) towards the acquirement of 'popular' cultural capital through discussions of football fandom – even if those discussions were perceived to be muted in relation to their working-class counterparts. Conversely, participants claiming to have been part of a working-class youth culture tended to display a more intense outlook on the practice of football, perceiving themselves to have invested more time and energy into football per se, as a 'serious leisure activity' rather than a pleasurable pastime (Jones 2000). Additionally, with less interest expressed in those fundamental sites associated with the acquisition of official cultural capital (for example, education), the unofficial or popular genre was deemed more important to the lives of the participants in terms of identity and perceptions of worthy competencies that are shared amongst peers.

To summarise: the initial part of this chapter demonstrates how participants present different experiences of football fandom genesis. Furthermore, whilst those experiences were connected in part to self-perceptions of class, it is important to raise the point that class-based arguments are not as straightforward as they may initially seem. As Pascale (2008: 357) illustrates 'if class was once marked and readable through the symbolic language of class habitus, today it is less often the case'. Thus, it is only when we look beyond the direct consumption experience of football fandom and into the various other consumer pastimes that participants simultaneously share with their peers, that we begin to understand the intricacies of applying notions of class to late modern fandom.

Beyond Football Fandom: Taste and Social Networks

In an infrequent but important scholarly contribution to the sociology of sport literature, Bourdieu (1978: 838) suggests that some leisure activities are closed to certain agents and that, consequently, this has implications for identifying and explaining the leisure activities of specific class groups:

> To understand how ... distinctive sports, such as golf, riding, skiing or tennis ... are distributed amongst the ... dominant classes ... it is the hidden entry requirements, such as family tradition and early training, and also obligatory clothing, bearing and techniques of sociability which keep these sports closed to the working classes and to individuals rising from the lower-middle and even upper-middle classes; and secondly because economic constraints define the field of possibilities and impossibilities without determining within it an agents positive orientation towards this or that particular form of practice (Bourdieu 1978: 838).

It would seem to follow then, that forms of leisure consumption are indicative of class position, yet this trend was not representative for the current sample of late modern football fans. It was not unusual to find that participants were actively engaged in other leisure/consumer practices (and other spectator sports) with diverse histories of class participation. Accordingly then, the increased access to eclectic leisure practices (from members of the current sample) renders such activities less as markers of class distinction than Bourdieu might have envisaged. Participant, Andy illustrates this point:

> Andy: I've got my horse racing friends and my football friends and I play golf sometimes as well ... I love my horse racing ... We all get dressed up you know, have a few glasses of wine in the enclosure and get pissed together. It's totally different from football, I mean it's the other end of the scale isn't it?... I feel at home at both ... I can mix in both circles, no problems. [Newcastle, aged 50 (MF)]

'Taste', in this instance, extends notions of class when Andy suggests that action is the product of personal choice, albeit with the added influence of peers. Consequently he draws on personal experience that celebrates a diversity of activities amongst friends. Perhaps then it is reasonable to suggest, as Hennion (2007: 103) does, that 'taste is lived by each but fashioned by all ... a history of oneself permanently remade together with others'. In contrast to Bourdieu,

Hennion acknowledges that influential acquaintances can have an eclectic (for example, not necessarily class specific) array of experiences to draw from. As such, football was not an exclusive leisure pursuit that participants used to characterise components of self. For instance, participants like Neil and Tina (below) express a desire to experience contrasting consumer practices within their leisure time and moreover, they were conscious not to restrict themselves to a narrow class-based existence:

> Neil: I like going to football for the craic. The songs, shouting at the ref [referee] and such, but on the other hand I love going to rugby because it gives you something different. It's more civilised … You get served your drinks on a tray at your seat. It's altogether more civilised. [Sunderland, aged 19 (STH)]

> KD: You seem to enjoy both sports but for different reasons. Is this accurate?

> Neil: Well, yeah. It's good to do different things, to have different strings to your bow. But yeah it's a different experience … Before you go to the game you kind of know what is acceptable and what isn't and you just go with the flow. At a rugby match there's a bit more respect for everything really.

> Tina: I've got different sets of friends all over the country who I do different things with … Yes, I would say that I come from a working class background but that doesn't mean that I'm going to eat egg and chips all my life – if you know what I mean. [Middlesbrough, aged 25 (MF)]

These quotations (above) highlight two points that are worthy of explanation (1) The importance of peer groups or social networks in the creation of multifaceted, but ultimately consumer based lifestyles and (2) The ability of agents to adapt to the conventions of diverse consumer practices. In the first instance, taste is as Hennion (2007: 104) states, 'pragmatic', often depending on more diverse friendship networks rather than traditional class groupings. Kate (below) is indicative of this. She explains: 'I support my friends in their activities and they come to the pub with me to watch football as well'. For Kate, all consumption practices are shared and are therefore not entirely individually motivated. She continues:

> Kate: So, like, we get involved in each other's activities … I started going to kickboxing with my friend Helen, Badminton with Amy, a group of us go to the Gym, the cinema and Nando's and stuff. So we just proper support each other. Because they're all from like different backgrounds and stuff, I do so many things that would never have crossed my mind … but its good fun finding

new interests and like, sharing them … My friends are lush. [Middlesbrough FC, aged 18 (MF)]

Furthermore, to say that taste is pragmatic does not negate the presence of habitual or objective forces. For instance, Giddens (1991: 81) speaks of a late modern lifestyle which can be identified as a more-or-less integrated set of practices that agents embrace, not only because such practices fulfil utilitarian needs, but because they give material form or a sense of routine to a particular narrative of identity that has past, present and future properties based on social interactions with peers. As a further point, the comments provided by Andy, Neil, Tina and Kate (above) signify an eclectic array of consumption behaviours that are simultaneously acted out by agents across a variety of dissimilar practices. Thus, the diverse nature of consumption practice further emphasises the pragmatic nature of taste per se, given that agents were able to morph, or change character, in accordance with the demands of multiple practices and associated peer groups. For example, Neil (above) attends both football and rugby matches and accepts that 'abusing the referee' is acceptable and fun within the practice of football fandom. Yet he insinuates that this is not acceptable, nor does he desire to do so, within the practice of spectator rugby. Moreover, Andy (below) understands those social differences that exist between modes of consumption (in terms of practice-specific etiquette when attending both football and horse racing) and yet he describes capabilities of adapting to the conventions of each practice. Sometimes he moves simultaneously from one to the next:

Andy: Saturdays can be busy and quite complex for me … . Earlier this year I went to a race meet at Gosforth race course but Newcastle were playing on Setanta[4] as well. So for most of the day I was all suited up and then at 5pm I got a taxi to mine [home], quick change, and then into the town with the lads to watch the match. [Newcastle United, aged 50 (MF)]

Being able to adapt to the conventions of any given practice (in this way) illustrates the potential that agents possess to act outside of limited structural genres. As Giddens (1991) highlights, lifestyles are open to change, though agents are only as reflexive as far as past histories, daily routines and future social networks will allow. Here, emphasis is placed on the importance of structure in both the reproduction and evolution of lifestyle practices:

---

4 The participant is referring to Setanta Sports (Great Britain), a sports media company that went into administration on 22 June 2009. All channels have ceased operations in Great Britain.

> Lifestyle is not a term that has much applicability to traditional cultures, because it implies choice within a plurality of possible options, and is adopted rather than 'handed down'. Lifestyles are routinised practices … but routines are reflexively open to change. (Giddens 1991: 81)

Giddens (above) accounts for lifestyles that are in one sense habitual (that is, they lead from structural forces) and yet, when confronted with new information or when agents come into contact with peers with diverse tastes, they have the capacity to reflect on and change behaviours. Indeed, based on one's breadth and depth of social networks, participants such as Kate and Tina (above) display symptoms of what has become known as 'omnivore' type behaviour. To make clear, the concept of the 'cultural omnivore' was originally used by Richard Peterson (1992) to explain the irregularities that exist between traditional theories of distinction and new research findings (Peterson and Simkus 1992). He explains that:

> … to our great surprise, those in high-status occupations were … more likely than others to report being involved in a wide range of lower-status activities, while respondents in the lowest status occupations were most limited in their range of cultural activities' (Peterson 2005: 259).

With this, Peterson implies that agents holding a high social status were not averse to participating in consumption practices associated with lower orders. In other words, they were cultural omnivores in the sense that they have a 'taste for everything' and more importantly, he argues that this has replaced the old arrangement where elite status was associated with snobbery (Warde, Wright and Gayo-Cal 2008). So, in the face of previous literature that has tended to focus on social elites (for example, working on the premise that working class groups are less omnivorous), it is now widely conceived that openness to diversity is valued by most people (Warde and Gayo-Cal 2009). The implications of this, according to Peterson (2005), indicate that the cultural omnivore is, perhaps, more suited to a late modern world with less distinct boundaries and a global inclusivity which is respectful of diversities (also see Peterson 1997, Hooker 2003).

In addition, whilst the presence of the cultural omnivore can be suggestive of an era that prizes choice and therefore individualisation, it is worth noting that findings from recent research indicate something altogether different. For instance, some researchers claim that structural conditions have an impact on omnivore status. Warde and Gayo-Cal (2009: 142) for example, propose that 'household structure, region, ethnicity, social connections, age, class and educational qualifications all contribute to explaining omnivoreness by volume'. Social class mobility has also been cited within the literature as a possible cause for omnivore increases (Trienekens 2002, Emmison 2003, Stuber 2005). This holds true for the following participant, and yet it is worth noting that perceptions of class mobility can cause high levels of anxiety for the upwardly mobile football fan like Peter (below). To explain – on interview, participant Peter had difficulty categorising himself into any particular class grouping, not for a lack of understanding, but rather as a consequence of what he concedes to be, a 'growing ambiguity between class groups'. With respect to his affiliation with football fandom, he recalls mixing with his working-class peers and he calls to mind: 'we were all rough and it was brilliant you know, but now things have changed for me'. Here, Peter specifically refers to his post-school education, concomitant profession and its related impact on perceptions of class and associated consumer experiences. He states:

> Peter: But like, now I'm a teacher, so it's difficult … Teacher is of course traditionally middle class. I don't really fit in with that group but I probably have a slightly better education than kids lower down the class rung. So they think that you are 'hoity toity' so you don't fit in so well there either. Then again, traditionally middle class kids that have been to private school are at totally different reference points. But if you go further down you get involved in a whole host of different reference points, so I think that I fit in a really uncomfortable position in terms of having a class identity, and like some of the people I think I've got most in common with, well they see me as a bit different. [Middlesbrough, aged 32 (STH)]

Notwithstanding the point that strict boundaries towards indicators of class are blurred and agents have more options to take part in a wider variety of consumer activities, feelings of distinction and uneasiness exist for the upwardly-mobile agent (for example, Peter) who must balance childhood tuition with a profession that has few social or historical reference points that are consistent with his childhood habitus. In addition to this, it is also true that blurred boundaries make for diverse friendship networks which increase the uni-directional flow and repertoire of consumption practices between and within traditional groupings. Peter explains:

> Peter: … I've gotten quite a few lads and lasses interested in football actually … I think that's what happens isn't it? When you meet different people throughout your life that are from different backgrounds you influence each other in certain ways, but like, its mainly to do with your hobbies. Like saying 'what did you do at the weekend sort of stuff', and then you end up inviting them, saying, 'you should come', and it sort of goes from there.

Despite those fluid and variable experiences between participants, the consumption of knowledge through sociability with peers was a constant aspect of fandom genesis as agents began to learn the game, albeit with different social connotations. Respondents emphasised that consuming football was a natural process for them, given their life situation as growing children within a specific, peer inspired environment. However, those experiences were predominantly offered as secondary, since for many participants, football fandom was learned at home and then practiced with peers.

Football Fandom, Habitus and the Role Of Family/Kin Groups

> You think you love some things, but no, it's your milieu, your origin, your formation that makes you appreciate them. (Hennion 2007: 103)

The most commonly cited and forcefully argued reason provided by participants for the consumption of football and therefore, for the genesis of uni-directional passionate support for one particular team, was the influence of a family member – predominately, but not always 'Dad'. In agreement with Hennion (above [advocating the influence of field and habitus]), participants such as Dave (below) draw attention to the possibility that fandom might be constructed by significant others and then unconsciously adopted as though it is an inherent component of one's being:

> Dave: People often say, 'I was born black and white' [team colours of Newcastle United], but that's not strictly true is it? You learn it at home, don't you? From your family. [Newcastle United, aged 40 (STH)]

As a direct influence on the future behaviour of children, family members were observed in this capacity to exert authority on others. That is to say, in the course of everyday interactions with significant others, the authoritative positioning of the parent can be used to heavily influence momentary and future actions of a child. Giddens (1984: 84-92) describes this phenomenon as the use and implementation of 'authoritative resources' in the sense that kin relationships are based on 'mutual positioning', and likewise, Bourdieu refers to the modelling of values, dispositions and practices of significant others – leading to the relative reproduction of previous generation habitus. In either instance the emphasis placed on the importance of tuition in the process of learning was reflected through the accounts of the respondents. Given the frequency of this occurrence, two varied but ultimately similar accounts are offered below:

Lisa: ... through my dad. My dad's a big Darlington fan, just kind of got forced into being amongst the crowd, gathering the experience. It's a family tradition ... I guess I was born into it. [Darlington, aged 20 (STH)]

Luke: Part of it is hereditary. It's your place of birth you know. My granddad went. My granddad took my dad and things like that. So, it's passed down, but you're not forced to do it. You want to! [Hartlepool, aged 21 (STH)]

The role of tuition, or at least deliberate exposure to the practice, is clearly evident within the responses cited above, but what remains unclear is whether fandom is a voluntarily (chosen by a reflexive agent) or involuntarily (forced onto a passive subject) practice. Furthermore, when interpreting those accounts (above) care must be taken not to overemphasise the literary structure of the evidence (Cavicchi 1998, Hills 2002). For instance when Lisa (above) refers to 'forced' fandom, she is in fact speaking in the context of a positive relationship with her father through football. This is something that the participant values, and as such, it ought not to be construed as force against one's will. In this instance, the adjective 'force' is used to dramatically portray the process of fandom origins (in light of Cavicchi 1998) and yet beyond surface level interpretation it implies a form of consented coercion, or the will to explore a practice that is important to significant others. Consequently there are more similarities than differences between the accounts of Lisa and Luke (above). Luke maintains that football fandom was passed down through kin relationships but it was not forced. Social agents, he asserts, would choose to continue and develop themselves within the practice, irrespective of kin relationships. So where Lisa indicates that she was 'forced' or 'coerced' into the practice, the opposite was noted by Luke (below). He maintains that football fandom was passed down through kin relationships but it was not forced. Social agents, he asserts, would choose to continue and develop themselves within the practice, irrespective of kin relationships:

Luke: How could it be forced? They might pass the baton on, but then you go in your own direction sort of thing ... I'm certainly not a clone of my dad when it comes to football, though I am grateful for the introduction. [Hartlepool, aged 21 (STH)]

Given the appreciation granted by both participants towards the role that parents play within fandom initiation, it seems that the concepts of 'force' versus 'choice' are, in the end, irrelevant within the minds of the subjects. Theoretically speaking, however, this issue is particularly useful as a means of thinking beyond the subjectivist-objectivist split, in order to help reveal the intricacies of football fandom cultures.

Conscious Coercion or Passive Acceptance?

Congruent with Bourdieu (1984) and Giddens (1984) it is clear that participants draw heavily on pre-understanding experiences or ones inherited background to make sense of their current involvement within football culture. What is unclear, however, is the extent to which those experiences are deliberately/intentionally influenced by significant others. In order to address this issue I turn to the accounts of those participants in the current sample who now have children of their own and so were able to draw on their experience as parents within this process. For instance, parents often spoke with enthusiasm and ultimately with pride about the ways in which they consciously attempt to pass on knowledge, tradition and love for football in ways reminiscent of their own fandom experiences:

> Tim: I got our Richard into it, one-hundred and twenty per-cent … Kitted him out in all the gear you know, made him feel part of it all. He was a mascot for Teesside Polly when he was six. He picked this up and became a Boro fan. Now he goes to away games, but he picked this up from his dad. [Middlesbrough, aged 54 years (MF)]

Likewise, participant Sarah[5] recalls the period when she introduced football spectatorship to her daughter. She reveals 'Before my daughter was born me and my husband went to every home and away match; so when she was old enough I took her to The Riverside.[6] Our passion rubbed off on Clair, we taught her the ropes and she's as mad as me now'. Narratives like these illustrate the recursive nature of fandom genesis in process, leading to collective participation, acquisition and consumption of fan specific knowledge. Indeed, when discussing the myths and realities of Millwall fandom, Robson (2000: 169) uses this argument (derived from Bourdieu 1977) to explain that practical mastery becomes embedded in the very perceptions and dispositions of fans (via teachings) to such an extent that actions are simply known in practice as 'the way things are done'. Actions and thought processes become ritualistic and exist in individuals as an awareness of what is appropriate in any given context. Crawford (2003) reports comparable findings with regard to the acquisition of knowledge and the adaptations that must be made (if particular practices are to thrive) as fans reach differing stages of 'career'. He suggests that time and space can alter type and intensity of fandom in the same way that careers change and develop over a life course. In the current context and with specific reference to parental influence it is possible to visualise a change in role as one

---

5 Sarah [Middlesbrough, aged 42 (MF)].

6 The Riverside is the stadium home of Middlesbrough FC. It was opened in 1995 to replace the previous stadium, Ayresome Park.

evolves, or perhaps more accurately, develops along a career path of football fandom: from the inducted to the inductor; apprentice to mentor; or student to teacher. However, whilst most parents (like those above) were consciously aware of their role within the process, others were more resistive to this notion:

> Dougie: I wouldn't say that it was forced on them. No. I mean, I tell them that I love Sunderland and if they have a similar passion I will be happy to take them. But I suppose they just want to spend time with their dad, and the only live football on offer is Sunderland. I've enthused them but I never bought them any Sunderland stuff to begin with. I think a nephew of mine bought a Sunderland shirt for my son when he was a baby, so it was other people rather than me instilling this. Then my daughter felt left out so we had to go and buy her one. And since then they have wanted to update to the next one. So it wasn't me initially, but I'm happy to keep that rolling over. [Sunderland, aged 37 (STH)]

Notwithstanding this, it is worth pointing out certain parallels between Dougie's self-evaluation of his parental influences and recollections of what childhood fandom was like for him. Dougie recalls the time spent with his father as 'an exciting learning curve' but insists that fandom was not forced:

> Dougie: I don't think he tried to instil Sunderland on me ... But he always used to take me if I wanted to go, and when I played he always used to drive us backward and forwards, so without forcing the issue he kept my passion burning.

The parity between accounts of childhood and parental roles lends support to the idea that the unconscious acquisition of child fandom can be later, 'consciously' or 'semi consciously', passed on to the future generation in an active and reciprocal manner. It seems reasonable to suggest that as football has taken root within society it has become an important aspect of family or kin tradition which continues to thrive in this sense. Yet, it must be noted that despite an abundance of supporting evidence, late modern society offers no guarantees that coercion will gain the desired effect or that tradition will roll over in such a predictable manner. Note the following examples:

> KD: Is your son a football fan?

> Dave: No, no! I can't stand it [laughing]. I've tried, I've tried! Maybe it's for the best after all the torture it's brought me over the years. No. He's got other interests. He goes paintballing, does things like climbing, outdoors adventure stuff, but he couldn't care less about Newcastle. [Newcastle, aged 40 (STH)]

Andy: Our Matty shows no interest really, he's into other things you know. He's massively into art and stuff. That's what he wants to do. I don't know where he gets it from. It's certainly not me or his mother. [Newcastle, aged 50 (MF)]

Thus, previous references to the power of objective structures (although conspicuous by number), ought not to be overemphasised. Yet again, those accounts provided (above) illustrate a less defined structure of acceptable leisure pursuits within kin groups, where next generation children can display a reflexivity which defies tradition. Here, it is worth pointing out that there are vast and various other routes through which the initiation of football fandom can occur and this is where the current findings break from the notions expressed in Bourdeiu's logic of practice. To explain, agency, for Bourdieu, operates within broader systems of constraint of which the individual is routinely unaware. Consequently it is bounded, compromised and accentuated by habitus (Adams 2006) and as Jenkins (1992: 77) contends, it 'hardly makes for reflexive agency in any meaningful sense of the word'. Moreover, this would suggest that reflexivity is as much the habitual outcome of field requirements as any other disposition and yet, given that participants in this sample demonstrate an ability to break free from the habitual requirements of the field, it would seem that one's capacity for reflexivity can extend beyond Bourdieu's logic of practice in certain instances.

Perhaps then, as Sweetman (2003: 535-6) suggests, there is a case for a potential hybridisation between Bourdieu's habitus and other accounts of reflexivity. To be specific, Sweetman acknowledges that Bourdieu's non reflexive habitus depends on relatively stable social conditions or a more simple, organised form of modernity that, he suggests, no longer exists in this manner. Furthermore, Sweetman and others (Adkins 2002, Craib 1992) insist that changes to the late modern environment have summoned conditions via which the 'reflexive habitus' has become increasingly common in the sense that uncertainty and change are paradoxically becoming a familiar occurrence in most fields – with agents possessing a greater tolerance of and taste for diversity. Consequently, agents have the capacity to change their position, for example, to refute parental advances, or where no family interest in football resides, they have the capacity to break the mould. At any stage of life, social actors can become football fans or alternatively opt out of the practice altogether. In other words, they are reflexive thinkers and during the course of their lives they are presented with various options to reproduce social action, or else change behaviour. And while they are indeed influenced by the consumption of core knowledge gathered through ones childhood habitus, they are also capable of consuming new knowledge of distant or estranged practices via interaction with others. Several subjects were demonstrative of this point:

Carol: My ex-hubby was a big football fan so it was always on in the house. I used to hate the game but learned to love it. Once I knew the rules, appreciated the skills and tactics and experienced the atmosphere I was hooked. [Hartlepool, aged 43 (STH)]

Removed from the influence that significant others have on one's consumption experiences (see above), participant Wanda (below) also provides details of a life estranged from football until one chance meeting with a friend at college. She explains how her mother had never encouraged involvement in football (believing that it was a game for hooligans) but in 2005 an external opportunity to attend a football match presented itself:

Wanda: In 2005 I had just gone to college and made new friends when one girl that I was in the same class with won a competition for a free box at Darlington for ten people and she invited me to go. I didn't really know what to expect, but that was it. I haven't looked back since. [Darlington, aged 21 (STH)]

The examples presented here demonstrate the role that new interactions can play in order to change life direction and consequently provide opportunities for agents to engage with distant or estranged consumer practices (adding to those habitual forms of learning previously documented). As my participants demonstrate, agents are constrained to an extent, but are not imprisoned by pre-understandings. Other examples of fandom genesis were equally non-conventional. That is to say, participant narratives displayed openness to influential modes of established and emergent technology which, for some, have unlocked the door to football fandom. For instance, when asked 'how did fandom begin for you'? Participant Richie[7] answered: 'Ian Rush.[8] I used to worship him when I was little, so I used to support the team he played for type of thing … Watched him on TV banging in the goals and followed him from there'. Beyond the allures of television, computer gaming was also shown to have influenced the onset of fandom for the following participant:

Ian: My story's a bit strange. I got into football in my late teens and I had never played football; was never on the school team or anything like that. My support began when I was introduced to Champ Manager[9] on the PC. I got to know all the current players, their values [economic value], how good they were and

---

7 Richie:[Liverpool, aged 32 (MF)].

8 Ian Rush was a football player for Liverpool FC and also a Welsh international throughout the 1980s and early 1990s.

9 The term 'Champ Manager' refers to computer games in the popular 'Championship Manager' series of association football simulation games. The game was originally written

all that stuff … It fast tracked my subject knowledge if you like [laughing]. We used to bring our teams into college [using paper printouts] and discuss our careers and that. It was totally addictive, and of course crossed over into reality, and that's what we did. That's when I started following football more generally. [Darlington, aged 26 (MF)]

Those experiences cited above are illustrative of an additional but no less important set of interactions and consumption experiences which have the potential to initiate fandom. Through the use of what Giddens terms 'allocative resources' including television (a resource which infiltrates any number of practices), or computer gaming (a late modern development of similar stature) it seems that para-social experiences can inspire social agents to alter behaviour. In the first instance, televised portrayals of celebrity athletes, such as ex-Liverpool Football Club player Ian Rush, have stimulated Richie (born to a working-class family of Newcastle United fans) to become a long-term supporter of Liverpool Football Club. Furthermore, this respondent was not alone in his behaviour. Football players Bobby Moore, Alan Shearer, Paul Gascoigne and Bernie Slaven were all noted to have had a similar effect on some of the respondents. Whilst some might argue that this is a form of 'celebrity fandom' and not 'football fandom' per se, it is important to note that, similar to the findings of Sutton, McDonald, Milne and Cimperman (1997), all respondents were loyal and committed to the team that the celebrity athlete represented at the time of their initiation into the practice. Thus, they remained a fan of the club, in spite of the celebrity athlete, club success, or the absence of it:

KD: Would you say then, that you were attracted to key individuals?

Stuart: Yes and no, because I stuck with West Ham since then. I mean, the Hammers have had a lot of disappointment so if I was interested in the stars [football celebrities] I would support Man U or Chelsea or something. I would say that most fans are not glory fans, but glory fans are just more visible because they follow high profile teams. [West Ham, aged 45 (MF)]

Stuart makes a point that previous academic research has tended to miss. Scholars seem to be in a hurry to explain how social life is rapidly changing rather than giving space to those stable features that remain, and to an extent, maintain social life (Giddens 1984). For instance, the race to explain change within the practice of football fandom has encouraged researchers to study fans of a handful of 'super clubs' (See King 1997, Sandvoss 2003) and consequently,

---

by Paul and Oliver Collyer (co-founders of Sports Interactive) in September 1992 and released onto the Amiga and Atari ST computer. It was released for PC soon after.

they have missed the more common examples that most typify everyday fandom. Moreover, fans (Stuart) emphasise the need to support the team irrespective of its fortunes (Giulianotti 2005) and thus, whilst the genesis of fandom (for example, in the case of Stuart and Richie) cannot be described as 'traditional', it retains those associated components of duty to support, albeit for a team that for all intents and purposes ought to exist outside of one's habitus.

Similarly, and with reference to participant Ian's (above) experiences with computer gaming, it is clear that over the course of the last 30 years, gaming has become a predominant feature of consumption and is now incorporated into patterns of everyday living (Crawford 2006). Furthermore, whilst Crawford and Gosling (2005) have been able to demonstrate a level of crossover between sporting and digital gaming interests and practices (in line with Bourdieu's habitus), the digital game 'Championship Manager' (CM) had an additional use for participant Ian. As Thornton (1995) illustrates, the media can be used in an informative capacity, and likewise computer gaming was used by this participant to rapidly gain the knowledge needed in order to initiate and maintain an interest in live football per se. Similar to Jenkins (2002), who indicates that gamers actively discuss the games that they play in social settings, Ian too draws on his experiences with CM to construct stories and narratives away from the games themselves. Moreover, given that CM deals with semi-factual knowledge regarding the practice of football fandom, it became an intense, enjoyable and invaluable way for this subject to learn about football culture as an adult without prior experience in the traditional sense.

Thus far I have argued that the genesis of football fandom is neither an entirely 'agency-' nor 'structure-driven' phenomenon given that our respondents have cited elements of both, sometimes simultaneously within recollections of early fandom experiences. The strength of the supporting evidence relating to the influential force of habitus is not in question, but it is the extent of the overriding usefulness of this concept, given the conditions endured by agents in the late modern period which requires further review. Hence, evidence of eclectic consumer lifestyles which are located above the level of habitus have contributed to a situation where leisure practices (including football fandom) have lost their cultural distinctiveness and this too, I argue, has affected the perceived coherence of football fandom in late modern life.

Constructing 'Other': Fluid and Variable Classifications of Fandom

For many of the participants, defining football fandom was a relatively difficult task and consequently many felt more comfortable categorising what football fans ought not to be:

KD: How would you define football fandom?

Bill: Emm. That's tricky. No one has ever asked me that before … emm, I can tell you what football fans shouldn't be if that's any use? [Sunderland, aged 34 (MF)]

Hence, self-perceptions of football fandom practice were based on fluid and variable differentiations that were inevitably defined or marked out via patterns of consumption. In agreement with Fiske (1992), evidence suggests that fans (like Bill above) are shown to differentiate fiercely the boundaries between what falls within perceptions of fandom and what does not. Moreover, boundaries were varied between fans of the same team in addition to expected distinctions between fans of different teams. So, in opposition to the findings of Jones (2000), who predicts a coherent account of football fandom within clear confines (for example, specifically relating to in and out groups), the current findings are characterised by internal fluidity (and therefore 'disharmony') which displays in composition the complex and eclectic nature of the late modern fandom base:

Tim: It's a total mix isn't it? Other than support for the team I'm not sure that they would even speak to each other on a social basis if they weren't wearing the colours … Fans aren't really united because they're so varied as people. [Middlesbrough, aged 54 (MF)]

By emphasising the potential disharmony of football fandom as a whole, Tim's assertion works against theorists who have previously implicated sport and leisure into processes of social distinction. For instance Veblen (1925), Bourdieu (1978) and more recently, Hargreaves (1986), Horne et al. (1999), Cashmore (2000) and Coakley (2008) have all specified that sports can be used as an indicator of social stratification. Most famously Bourdieu (1978: 820) asks:

… according to what principles do agents choose between different sports activities or entertainments which in any given moment in time are offered to them as being possible?

Within the answer to this rhetorical question Bourdieu argues that class differences and associated cultural capital exist between genres of sport (for example, between boxing and golf) and furthermore he categorically positions spectator football as a popularist, vulgar practice set within a definite and clear cultural realm:

… the probability of watching one of the reputedly most popular sporting spectacles such as football … declines markedly as one rises in the social hierarchy. (828)

Bourdieu uses the word 'vulgar' to imply that the combined popularisation of spectator football (that is, a game for the majority of people and hence a 'prol sport') and the associated values/virtues are enough to repel the upper echelons of society from partaking in this practice. This assertion may have been appropriate at the time of writing (for example, specifically with reference to problems of football hooliganism in the 1970s) but Bourdieu was not yet privy to those rapid changes to football culture that would unfold in the years following this publication emanating from a mix of exogenous and endogenous factors (some of which are detailed in Chapter 2). Indeed, contrary to Bourdieu's theory of distinction, sociological studies within the 1990s and into the twenty-first century were more concerned with the bourgeoisification of football fandom rather than clear lines of cultural distinction between sporting practices (Crabbe and Brown 2004, Moor 2007).

Notwithstanding this point, the reference to vulgarity has not entirely disappeared within the current data set, though the context of its use has changed shape to resonate more sharply with the work of Douglas (1966). The eclectic backgrounds of self-proclaimed football fans are such that uncertainty of cultural distinction has resulted in internal interpretations of differentiation based on authenticity claims and notions of otherness, or what Douglas (1966) would describe as perceptions of 'dirt'. For Douglas, human tendency dictates that one will attempt to fix or examine the behaviour of others in relation to one's own experiences. Thus, any behaviour that occurs outside of routine actions (common to the agent in question) will create disruption, ambiguity and can be transcribed negatively as a threat to one's ontological security. It is in those situations, Douglas argues, that boundaries of otherness are drawn and perceptions of dirt are formed. She states:

Uncleanness or dirt is that which must not be included if a pattern is to be maintained. (1966: 40)

In a similar manner to the concept of habitus, Douglas proposes that cultures and sub-cultures contain values and behavioural patterns which are impossible to escape. Here she raises the possibility that any behaviour considered as 'other' will be perceived negatively as agents begin to condemn and therefore distance themselves from those behaviours (Douglas 1966: 38). On such grounds (that is, those proposed by Douglas) I now discuss the variable characterisations of football fandom that were made by this sample of participants. More specifically, I demonstrate how it is that modes of consumption define and sustain boundaries of otherness for football fans. Discussions begin with an account of 'fake fandom'.

Characterising Fake Fandom

Fake fandom was one dominant idea of otherness pursued by most interviewees. This was expressed using an array of vernacular (based on personal experiences) and yet lack of loyalty was constant and definitively present in the construction of 'fake'.

> Sarah: The Boo Boys! They get on the players backs which I don't think is a good thing to do. It doesn't help the team so why do it? As a supporter it's your role to support, so if you're not supportive just don't bother. That's my attitude anyway. [Newcastle, aged 42 (MF)]

Sarah's account of otherness adds support to academic suggestions that conceptions of the fandom base as traditionally loyal are unwise because some are (that is, according to Sarah) more casual in their loyalties than others (Mahony, Madrigal and Howard 2000). Furthermore, as Hinch and Hingham (2005) have illustrated, authenticity is potentially more subjective and personal than some authors have previously thought. For example, participant Nats (below) concentrates attention on the conspicuous consumption of sport-related goods to explain the fake fan. She suggests that buying the latest merchandise (if considered in isolation) is not enough to gain acceptance or to qualify as a 'real fan':

> Nats: They say, 'oh, I support the Boro me' and come in all their kit. But when the team aren't playing so well they are like, 'we've had it, we're not coming here anymore'. They do my head in. [Middlesbrough, aged 24 (STH)]

The facetious emphasis placed on the observation that fans of this description 'come in full uniform' is used here by Nats to illustrate the perception of the fake supporter. In this instance the fake is someone who may attempt to blend in or pass themselves off as real by overtly consuming merchandise and yet their identity as fakes can be easily deciphered by more authentic, pure, non-polluted fans. Additionally, lack of consistency of support when combined with the purchasing of signifying merchandise was further acknowledged by Linda as a clear attempt by fake fans to lift their status amongst peers:

> Linda: … My boss for instance didn't used to go to the match until he got given a corporate ticket. He didn't even know if we had a game or not … Now he's covered head to toe in red and white, got all the accessories and genuinely thinks that he's the biggest supporter ever. Somehow he thinks he's proven his status as a supporter … People like this aren't what I consider real fans. You can tell them a mile off. [Sunderland, aged 30 (STH)]

Being able to 'tell them a mile off', as this participant explains, provides an assumption of authenticity based on the knowledge of the observer. Moreover, such illustrations coincide with Fiske (1992) when he indicates that it is knowledge which allows participants to see through that which is normally hidden to the uncultured eye, or in this instance, that which is inaccessible to the fake or non-fan. Take the following transcript extract as an additional example. The participant 'Gary' describes his disapproval of fans who are not able to reason out situations without depending on the simplified offerings sold by the mass media:

> Gary: Some fans think that anything they read in the paper or anything that commentators say is true, but often its bullshit and that's how dumb some fans are. They don't know anything. They don't properly understand the game, or situations that emerge, so, kind of their opinion is the same as the media's. Proper fans have a real understanding ... You suspect just by looking at them but you can tell who fake fans are after two sentences of speaking with them. [Sunderland, aged 28 (MF)]

Such findings indicate that fan cultures are not coherent but are in fact sites of internal contestation based on type, extent and perception of consumption practice. Thornton (1995) writes similarly regarding the presence of differential statuses within and between sub-cultural groups. Through engagement with Bourdieu's (1984) work on distinction, Thornton coined the term 'sub-cultural capital' to discuss how dance club cultures are marked by a series of authenticity claims. Additionally, similar processes were noted here between football fans, although the route of achieving cultural capital was largely based on longevity and could not be bridged by economic resources alone:

> Lee: ... Fandom is open to anyone but it's not something that people can just acquire or buy or whatever. You've got to treat it seriously ... It becomes part of your make up, like it lasts a lifetime. [Middlesbrough, aged 24 (STH)]

Football fans inhabit a culture where authenticity is constantly scrutinised by themselves and others. Accordingly, fans are judged not only on what they do (that is, type and extent of consumption), but the perceived genuineness relating to performance. For instance, participant Nicola[10] is adamant that she would never lower herself to support any other team than that of her home town. She explains: 'I look at all of those glory supporters – like the ones born in East London that support Man United and I think – you need shooting you know;

---

10 Nicola:[Newcastle, aged 27 (MF)].

where's your self-respect?' Additionally, Matty makes comments regarding a sub-group of fans that he believes hold alternative motives for support:

Matty: I'll tell you what though, I hate those fuckers, those wannabe celebrities from the fanzines who crave the limelight and act as an authority on football fans. They're like fucking vultures just so as they can say 'look, I was on the telly'. [Middlesbrough, aged 32 (STH)]

In the examples above, the perceptions of otherness or dirt are controlled to an extent via a panoptic gaze (Foucault 1979). Football fans were the subjects of their own inward surveillance (or self-standards) and would constantly monitor the perceived value of authentic behaviours and those behaviours thought not to count as authentic. However, due to the fluid and variable nature of the supporter base, those standards or rules of panoptic governance were, in the end, so diverse (for example, depending on peer, kin groups) that no generic or coherent rules exist from which to judge authentic behaviour. As Wheaton (2007) suggests, studies of sport have illustrated that although sports sub-cultural groups have some shared values, the experiences of participants are not homogenous. Panoptic power, it seems, mainly exists in relation to tight kin or peer 'learning groups' and hence purity or authenticity of performance lies firmly in the eye of the beholder. Participant Carl[11] explains: 'to be honest, I don't like any of the fans apart from the ones who do what I do' and likewise Ruth indicates that she has an affiliation with only a small proportion of same group football fans:

Ruth: Likeminded fans are, like, those people that you grew up with. Those are the type of fans that you identify with. There's many others who support Boro that I don't have time of day for. [Middlesbrough, aged 42 (STH)]

When combined with the notion offered by Gary (for example, when he suggests that fakeness can be diagnosed by observing others) it is possible to unveil two potential sites from which fellow fans examine one another for purity of performance within the practice. First, and in line with Douglas (1966), results indicate a focus on the judgement of bodily dispositions which extend beyond the signifying appearance of clothing. Like Foucault (1979), Douglas explains that social structures are represented within the human body as social rules. Bourdieu too refers to this eventuality as 'bodily hexis', in the sense that bodily movements are highly charged with social meaning and thus provide clues to an agent's place within the game, their underlying habitus and concomitant position within the field.

---

11 Carl [Darlington, aged 23 (MF)].

Similarly, participants also used bodily signs to gage deserved status or capital within the practice. For instance, when asked 'how can you tell if a fellow fan is a fake without knowing them personally?' participant Darren[12] offered the following explanation: 'First, I would say that they don't think that they're fake; no one is going to admit that'. In this sense Darren suggests that there are many deluded fans who truly believe themselves to be authentic, but he insists that they do not have those social reference points that would help them to make a truly accurate judgement. He continues, 'They're called fake by people who have been around the game since they were little and can recognise a true fan when they see one. It's hard to say how you know but ... it's their actions. Like their trying too hard to fit in or something'. Gary provides support for this contention when he implies:

Gary: To be a fan is to act genuinely as any situation gets going, you know? Naturally is what I mean. You don't act over the top because you are comfortable in your own skin. You react to your feelings and the situation and not because a man with a microphone tells you to. [Sunderland, aged 28 (MF)]

For Gary, the performance of overt consumption – such as those marketing or entertainment ploys that are present on any given match-day (that is, reacting on cue to the match-day MC or waving at the big screen for Sky Sports television) – displays un-admirable attributes that equate to trying too hard. Participants have also articulated this message in various other ways, including explanations about how to detect fake fandom when watching televised football. In the examples presented below, both participants were interviewed in public house venues in central locations of Newcastle Upon-Tyne. In both instances the participants draw on live televised pictures of Sky Sports 'Super Sunday' matches (playing in the background of the interview) to animate and breathe life to their explanations:

Dave [*Participant refers to televised fans that are pointing and waving at themselves on the big screen whilst the game is in process*]

Now he's what I'd call a numpty [derogatory term], like what we are talking about; an example of fake. Loads of people like him are at the match watching the big screens, hoping to get on telly [television], rather than watching the football. Muppets aren't they? [Newcastle, aged 40 (STH)]

Rebecca [*Participant points to the television screen in the pub as football player Cesc Fabregas takes a corner kick*]

---

12 Darren [Newcastle, aged 45 (MF)].

See what I mean? If you watch a match like this and, say Fabregas goes to take a corner, like there, you can see all the flashes; all the blinding lights from cameras … They treat players like film stars. People seem to want to take away a souvenir of the day or something rather than watch the game. [Newcastle, aged 24 (MF)]

In both instances the respondents have made reference to the manner that fandom is performed by fellow supporters. As well as documenting the changing nature of the live venue (for example, with the integration of consumer experiences such as the big screen) and the noticeable presence of 'tourist' type behaviour amongst fans, it is clear that even when watching football via the mass media fans hold expectations about how others ought to behave at the live event. For instance, feeling the need to resist the man with the microphone (Gary, above) or the lure of the big screen (Dave, above) each participant draws on what Giddens calls 'practical consciousness' in relation to perceptions of authenticity. In other words, agents immediately draw upon tacit modes of knowing how to behave or present themselves in the context of any given social practice (Giddens 1982).

Characterising Gendered Fandom

It is worthy of note that most female participants were comfortable expressing modes of otherness or behaviour that they consider as fake, but a significant proportion felt less secure and less comfortable about how they were perceived by others within the practice. Despite possessing levels of knowledgeability and competencies which ought to bolster social capital, many females felt that they had to consistently prove their status or capital in order to avoid the label of fake:

Wanda: People see me with a shirt on and think 'oh yeah'! It's only when they talk to you that they realise that you know what you are talking about, rather than just being a girl in a shirt. [Darlington, aged 21 (STH)]

Similarly, in his study of ice hockey fans, Crawford (2001) revealed that although half of the regular audiences at live matches were women, female supporters were often excluded from progressing into the highest echelons of this supporting community. Thus, in spite of the potential for reflexively in late modern lifestyles, it seems that some traditional barriers to inclusion remain. Like Giddens (1991) suggests, one should not forget that late modernity too produces difference, exclusion and marginalisation. Likewise, Kelly (below) indicates that female fans can often find that they are not taken seriously and therefore have more to prove to others within the practice:

Kelly: I'm not saying all, but some male supporters treat us differently. Most are cool but you always get the occasional guy who says like 'get your kit off for the lads' or even the ones that are sensible patronise you a bit by dumbing down opinions and such. They presume that because I'm a girl I won't quite follow what they are saying … They don't like it when I disagree with them and put my own valid points across. [Newcastle, aged 25 (MF)]

In addition to this, many more female fans were frustrated by the attitudes that were cast towards their overt behaviour during a match:

Clair: … when I go to football games I get like really quite into it and things and I shout. Now, it's alright if a man shouted it, but I just get like really dirty looks. I'm like 'why should I get them looks when it's just the same as when a lad shouts it'? [Middlesbrough, aged 23 (STH)].

Kelly and Clair (above) hold the view that female fans have to work harder to earn their place as authentic members of a fan group, often against a backlash of stereotypical masculine bravado which permeates down through all modes of fandom. For instance, in addition to negative experiences at the live venue, Tina (below) emphasises similar concerns within the virtual fan environment:

Tina: I entered a Vodafone 'Full on Fan' competition. When I got selected to go on the radio a few of the guys I know told me to go on the forums (interactive internet websites) and ask for people to vote for me, which I did, but the further I got in the competition the more comments were made about women and football … It seems my opinion isn't valid on that forum coz I'm a woman and they are knob heads … There's a woman on there who is accepted by them, but that's coz she has shagged half of them. [Middlesbrough, aged 25 (MF)]

Thus, a number of female fans have experienced what Muggleton (2000: 153) describes as 'the effects of core membership'. This evokes a masculine criterion and privileges the views of the established who tend always to be men. Additionally, given that the goal of many female fans was to fit into the practice as authentic supporters, one tactic used was to frequently apply knowledge of the game when in conversation with those suspected of doubting their credentials as authentic fans:

Suzi: When I was working with this guy he was calling me a plastic football fan [derogatory comment] and we ended up having a massive argument and he said for me to explain the offside rule and was surprised when I knew it. Then he just gives me a harder question and yeah I think people do frown upon you being a female football supporter but you've just got to show that you know your stuff. [Middlesbrough, aged 23 (MF)]

However, despite the presence of a siege mentality or a coherent response from female football fans as a reaction to posed questions of authenticity (for example, based on gender), it is worth noting that the same participants also displayed signs of in-gender disharmony more generally, with some casting blame on others for their contribution to this negative stereotype:

Rachel: I do think that some female fans do us no favours. Some of them tend to go in groups to ogle at the blokes and others stand there in sexy clothes with their tits out. That's how we get a bad press. [Sunderland, aged 28 (STH)]

Here Rachel indicates that certain groups of female fans have ulterior motives for following football, that is, as a tool for picking up boys or to worship attractive players. For Rachael, such behaviour will always fail to gain the acceptance of the 'male core' and thus she too turns her back against this 'inauthentic' form of female fan.

Characterising the Undesirables

Perceptions of otherness or dirt also exist beyond conceptions of fake, inadequate or inauthentic fandom. In addition, participants also made reference to wider ideas of social differentiation that were primarily based on type and extent of consumer behaviour. Consumption activities were used in order to condemn certain fan types that were perceived to have pushed the boundaries of normality (that is, behaviour that is perceived as normal by participants) both within and outside of football fandom practice. In the following extract I highlight one of many examples that demonstrate the unwanted presence of a particular type of undesirable group:

Jacko: Quite a large group of support, I guess, class themselves as 'the Toon Army', and the Toon Army is anyone who is probably uneducated or young. So you are talking about people from about sixteen to twenty-one and even kids in their early thirties or forties. You see them every day; you know they haven't moved on. They are the same old dirty chavs that they always will be. I call them 'The Cartoon Army'. [Newcastle, aged 28 (MF)]

Jacko explains that the 'Cartoon Army' is representative of a relatively new but momentarily popular form of social categorisation of otherness that is commonly coined 'the chav'.[13] It is important to note that the concept of otherness associated with the 'chav-fan' ought not to be confused with perceptions of fake fandom. In fact, unlike fakes, chav fans were praised for their dedication to the team via type and extent of monetary consumption. Indeed, Laura makes the following distinction:

KD: What is the major difference between the fake and the chav fan?

Laura: Chavs can't be knocked for their dedication, I mean they probably attend more away games than me, probably spend more money than me but it's just the way they go on. They're bad mannered and intimidating and probably have a lot in common with old school hooligans. Getting back to the Fake fans they are less intimidating but equally annoying. They're 'all show' and 'no substance' ... fur coat and no knickers as my granddad says ... He means that they lack the staying power of real fans. [Hartlepool, aged 20 (STH)]

So, chavs are perceived to be 'real fans' in the sense that they demonstrate a certain dedication to invest in, consume and share with others, a passion for the team. Yet, perhaps more than any other fan grouping, the chav-fan was most frequently mocked by the interviewees in this sample for a particular form of consumption practice that was considered to be vulgar. Moreover, whilst the reported vulgarity did not necessarily relate to football fandom per se, this concept was used by the participants to attribute superior social capital to the critical onlooker. This coincides with the work of Tyler (2008) when he underlines that the notion of disgust is often directed at the chav. Likewise, Miller (1997: 218) argues that disgust or dirt 'needs images of bad taste ... to articulate the judgements that it asserts'. In the current sample, this was played out through discussions relating to the conspicuous consumption of sportswear:

Paula: They are the ones that wear their Boro shirts regardless of where they go. The blokes are Burberry-wearing, greasy scum, covered head to toe in sportswear, and the girls, if you can call them 'girls', are Vicky Pollard,[14] Kappa Slapper types. [Sunderland, aged 32 (MF)]

---

13 In a historical context, Hayward and Yar (2006) have illustrated the escalating rate of media use relating to the term 'chav'. They report that there has been a rapid rise to public consciousness given that virtually zero references were to be found in national newspapers between 1995-2003, and yet 946 references were found during 2004-05 alone.

14 Vicky Pollard is a character from the popular satirical comedy series 'Little Britain' which aired on BBC. She is a teenage mother and juvenile delinquent, played by the character actor Matt Lucas.

'Chavness' is evidenced here to cause feelings of repulsion. Paula (above) refers to a number of signifiers (relating to excessive consumption) that have become synonymous with perceptions of the chav. Moreover, as Tyler (2008: 21) suggests, those signifiers are often used to epitomise bad taste:

> … perceptions of the chav are primarily identified by means of his or her "bad", "vulgar" and excessive consumer choices – cheap brands of cigarettes, cheap jewellery, branded sports tops, gold-hooped earrings, sovereign-rings, Burberry baseball caps.

Furthermore, Hayward and Yar (2006: 16) argue that the chav phenomenon 'recapitulates the discursive creation of the underclass', while simultaneously reconfiguring it within the space of commodity consumption. In other words, otherness becomes dependent on significations of 'taste', not in terms of what one can afford to buy, but rather the garish nature of what is perceived to be chav fashion and 'bad taste' more generally. This was expressed by participants in a number of ways and with a surprising amount of scorn and denigration. For instance, the following participant recalls an incident that took place on 12 September 2008 at St. James Park that is worth citing at length:

> Martin: I sat in the same seat for in excess of ten years and there was good camaraderie between us but there was also a real type of rivalry with the nob-head chavs that sat alongside us as well. We never kind of spoke to them coz we looked at them like 'you're a twat and you're an embarrassment to the club, and you're the type that will be outside of St. James next time there is a sky sports camera'. So there is a divide that is probably never talked about. I mean I sit in front of a kid that is a total chavy bastard, about five years younger than me. Turns up with his black and white shirt on all the time, like an advert for 'Sport Direct' but then protests about Ashley.[15] He's fucking thick. To sum him up, on the day of the Hull game when all of the demonstrations were going on there was also a small demonstration at three pm in line with kick-off, for some reason down near the Central Station. So that fucker rolled in at about twenty past three. He sat in his seat and goes 'That was fucking class, we were all walking the streets shouting Ashley out', I just turned to him and goes 'I'll tell you what it is, I wouldn't of fucking let you in me like'. He said 'what for'? I says 'the fucking team needed you at Three O' clock'clock, not at twenty past, I wouldn't of fucking showed me face. You want to fuck off and join the rest of

---

15 Mike Ashley was the owner of Newcastle United at the time of interview. The protests that this participant makes reference to were held by fans in response to the alleged 'forced' resignation of Kevin Keegan from his position as first team manager.

your pasty eating chav mates in Eldon Square. By the way could you be wearing more Ashley products?' He just didn't fucking reply. [Newcastle, aged 42 (STH)]

Here, Martin draws attention to the disharmony that can be felt between fans of the same team. Moreover he provides evidence to suggest that those fluid and varied positions are manifest through a particular way of seeing and evaluating overt consumption choices. Many participants (like Martin) were particularly hostile to the 'chav' contingent who were frequently blamed for damaging the reputation of respective football clubs through the high profile but low intellectual media coverage choreographed by Sky Sports News:

Alan: I think that everyone is embarrassed about the scenes outside of St. James Park. Largely, I think, orchestrated by Sky Sports who like to have pictures flashing around the country of knackers [derogatory term] standing outside the Gallowgate, and there's been no shortage of them. But it does embarrass us. It does present the wrong picture of what Newcastle United supporters are all about. [Newcastle, aged 29]

On the evidence presented, it seems reasonable to suggests that consumption practices tend to define boundaries of otherness for this sample of football fans in the following ways: (a) Fake fans are criticised for relentlessly consuming the latest fashionable football merchandise, but lacking any real emotional connection to the team; (b) Female fans were noted as material consumers, but were perceived to lack understanding associated with the consumption of football knowledge; (c) Finally, the chav-fan was praised for both emotional and financial commitment to the football team, however, the perceived vulgar nature of consumption habits (attributed to chavs) were mocked by all participants.

Characterising Togetherness

Despite fluid and variable differences noted 'within fandom groups', macro perceptions of solidarity and togetherness were also presented (if not equally) in the accounts of participants – adding to the complexity of the football fandom phenomenon:

Nats: Middlesbrough Football Club is definitely a big community. It is a community club and I think we're a good bunch of fans. [Middlesbrough, aged 24 (STH)]

Football fans were able to move with ease between concepts of micro and macro group identification and so, perceptions of difference and solidarity were mutually and nonsensically intertwined. It should be noted that reflections relating to solidarity, coherence or togetherness featured less in interviews with participants, but when used, they were heartfelt and were often inseparable from feelings of affection towards the home town or city of respective clubs:

> Kev: When someone says Newcastle, I think of the team, the lads, the fans. In many ways the team is the City though. That's our barometer. That's how we measure ourselves. [Newcastle, aged 23 (MF)]

With this it becomes apparent that the fragmentations of fandom that were described earlier in this chapter (based on perceptions of consumption acts and perceived authenticity of performance) can be traversed when agents reflect on the social and historical significance of the supported football club and its connection to local people within the geographical proximity of the club surroundings. When the subject was raised, participants were noted to speak in a manner that would transcend any notion of 'difference' that may resonate on a practical level:

> Colin: I know I've slaughtered some fans of this club, but in the end I am a proud fan and they're proud fans. A cheesy song they used to sing when we were in Europe 'just a small town in Europe'. We are a small town, a tiny town, and we are a good Premier League Club … We don't get as many fans but we're not going to, because of the size of the town. I've read somewhere that we have the most local fans in terms of ratio to the town and I take pride in that … approximately fifty per-cent of the residents of Middlesbrough go to the match and I think that's brilliant. The other fifty per-cent are no doubt watching elsewhere. One thing that Boro fans have got in abundance is pride in our team and pride in our town! [Middlesbrough, aged 53 (STH)]

Overall then, whether deconstructing fandom to suit 'micro group logic', or whether they create a temporary sense of 'macro community', the participants in this sample have built notions of identity and self-worth on their perception of consumption acts. Following this, and borrowing the term from Anderson (1991), I suggest that football fans ought to be thought of as 'imagined communities' of diverse consumers. Such imagined communities exist, not through political systems of power, but through the habitual teachings of kin groups and the influence of eclectic peer factions. Consequently perceptions of difference and sameness are extenuated through imagined communities and then expressed through cultural systems of taste and shared experiences of consumption.

Chapter 5
Consuming Corporate Values: Football Fandom Habitus, Disneyisation and Late Modern Life

... more and more aspects of our society are exhibiting features that are associated with Disney theme parks. (Bryman 2004: vii)

This chapter considers the effect that commercial institutions can have on the life habitus of late modern football fans. Focusing primarily on Alan Bryman's concept of 'Disneyisation' (see above quote), crucial questions about institutions and structures are raised under the assumption that football fans are undoubtedly affected by changes in marketing, advertising and delivery of commercial goods and services relating to practice (Horne 2006). Accordingly, in what follows I demonstrate how market processes have become inflected within the everyday lives of football fans to such an extent that they are now, in the minds of my participants, conceptually inseparable. Before further exploring this issue through the individual narratives of football fans, the initial part of this chapter draws briefly on Disneyisation as a theoretical construct for explanations of consumerism in late modern life.

Disneyisation as Theoretical Construct

As a scholarly term Disneyisation is a relatively new concept that was derived by Alan Bryman in 1999 though his is not the first account to suggest that late modern society is beginning to take on the characteristics of the global film and entertainment company 'Disney'. Scholars such as Schickle (1986), Walz (1998), Ross (1999) and Wasko (2001) have previously referred to a process of 'Disneyfication', often associated with sanitising materials (for example, fairytales or novels) by implementing a programmatic way of operating that transforms objects into superficial, simplistic and increasingly homogenous form. These authors (cited above) agree that 'to Disneyfy' is to adhere to a systematic recipe that ultimately serves to stifle individuality, magic, mystery and spontaneity in order to maintain a standardised, but commercially successful, format.

Accordingly, the term Disneyfication has become tainted with a largely negative view of the Disney company and its influence, rather than advancing a discussion relating to the wider impact of the emblematic aspects of its operations. Bryman (2004) opts to use the term 'Disneyisation' in an attempt to move beyond those negative connotations and, moreover, he draws attention to the underlying principles that Disney theme parks exemplify in order to illustrate concomitant effects on the economy, culture and social life more generally. Created on this basis Bryman uses the Disney theme park as a template to illustrate a series of increasingly common procedures that are taken to 'ensure the satisfaction of consumers and to offer new strategies for selling in post-Fordist times' (Horne 2006: 38). More specifically, the Disneyisation thesis gives space to the influencing power of marketing procedures and an increasing inclination to consume which generally takes into consideration four main components that encourage variety, choice and differentiation. Those components include: (1) Theming; (2) Hybrid Consumption; (3) Emotional Performative Labour and (4) Merchandising.

Theming makes up the initial component. It draws on the assumption that consumer enjoyment or dislike for a service is only partially conditioned by the objective quality of the service itself. The servicescape (for example, the contrived environment and ambience or the manner in which a service is delivered) is also thought to be a crucial factor of the consuming experience (Pine and Gilmore 1999). Furthermore, whilst typical elements of theming are external to the product or service (for example, restaurants that draw on well-known and accessible cultural themes such as music, sport, Hollywood movies, geography, history etc.), some company brands and logos 'become so distinctive that they grow to be themes in-themselves' (Bryman 2004: 18). Beardsworth and Bryman (1999) refer to such theming examples as 'reflexive' given that the theme, the brand and its expression are indistinguishable. In any instance, theming is part of a strategy of differentiation that is deployed in order to allow agents to lose themselves in a contrived experience that will encourage consumption.

The second feature, 'hybrid consumption' refers to the merging of forms of consumption associated with different institutional spheres. Those forms become interlocked in a deliberate attempt to create a destination that will hold consumer attention and encourage agents to spend more time and money in a particular space than they otherwise might. Walt Disney embraced this process when he realised at an early stage that Disneyland had great potential as a vehicle for selling food and various other goods (Bryman 2004). In some instances shops and restaurants were designed to merge seamlessly with the star attraction. The design of the Star Tours ride in three Disney theme parks for example, 'ensures that visitors walk through a shop containing Star Wars merchandise in order to reach the exit'

(Bryman 2004: 59). It is worth mentioning that the principles behind this design are not unique to Disney. In fact, Bryman points out that department stores, the high street and amusement arcades have always shown elements of hybridisation. However, the point he makes is that in late modern life, hybrid consumption has become more formulae and systematically used across the entire leisure sector.

As a third component, the concept of 'emotional labour' is used by Bryman to refer to a specific delivery of service that, if implemented effectively, can offer a source of differentiation. It is a means of distinguishing services that are otherwise identical in order to make the consumer experience memorable and the customer more likely to return. In Disney theme parks, for instance, employees are akin to performers that invest their time and energy to ensure that customers have a positive emotional experience. This logic is supported by research indicating that customers judge the success of any commercial exchange not only on the quality of product, but quality of service too (Henkoff 1994, Solomon 1998). On this basis Bryman suggests that fostering emotional labour to satisfy the needs of customers has become a crucial component of the framework of most businesses in the leisure sector.

Finally, 'merchandising' alludes to the promotion of goods bearing copyright images and logos. It is a form of franchising that leverages additional uses out of existing well-known images and whilst it too pre-dates the Disney theme park, Walt Disney was quick to realise the immense profitability that merchandising could bring to the company. According to Klein (1993) in the years immediately following the arrival of Mickey Mouse (arguably Disney's first major global success), over half of the studio's profits were attributable to merchandise and in the later years, scholars such as Forgacs (1992) suggest that the cuteness of cartoon characters was designed with merchandising in mind. Accordingly then, the key principle of merchandising is to extract further revenue from an image that has already attracted attention.

To reiterate, according to Bryman, Disneyisation does not only serve as a model for theme parks but for other leisure spaces such as shopping malls and the sport spectacle too. So, given that football is conceived of as an increasing sphere of consumer activity (Gray et al. 2007, Giulianotti 2002, Horne 2006, Sandvoss 2003), the following sections of this chapter explore the Disneyisation thesis from the perspective of football fans. By doing so, it is possible to discuss how processes of Disneyisation are received, interpreted and integrated into the life habitus of the late modern football consumer.

Theming and Football Fandom

Theming provides a veneer of meaning and symbolism to the objects to which it is applied ... In infusing objects with meaning through theming, they are deemed to be made more attractive and interesting than they would otherwise be. (Bryman 2004:15)

There is evidence to suggest that football fandom has evolved to contain a variety of 'themed experiences' that are used by commercial organisations in order to make various leisure opportunities more attractive. Drawing on the match-day theme, for instance, helps some leisure providers (such as public houses and bars) to connect to a passing trade audience. Conversely, from the perspective of the football fan, there are many lucrative offers to take advantage of:

Linda: Compared to what it used to be like, local businesses and like franchised pubs, shops and restaurants get on board with football don't they?

KD: How do you mean?

Linda: Well, there's a load to do in and around the stadium and loads of competition to get the punters in. They know [referring to leisure providers] that you will be meeting up with your mates or family before-hand so they tempt you with loads of promotions for food and drink; especially for the football crowd … We go wherever the best offer is on. [Sunderland, aged 30 (STH)]

By exercising consumer power, Linda selects the best offer from a pool of competing themed services that must remain fluid and flexible in response to market conditions and sensibilities of the football fan. As Bryman contends, theming works on the premise that consumers grow increasingly bored with standardised services and settings with which they are typically confronted. Therefore 'themed promotions' (like those inferred above) are often used to create a range of diverse experiences with the aim of attracting a wide demographic to the business and thus, to maximise income. Consequently, leisure providers use themed events (sometimes temporary in nature) as part of a fluid marketing strategy to capitalise on passing trade. Participants were certainly aware of this marketing strategy and were prepared accordingly:

Kirsty: When we travel to away matches, pubs in all city centres always put on match-day entertainment … By snuggling up to football, it becomes a football pub for a few hours but as soon as the match is over and the Saturday night crowd come to town you can't get in the same bar if you're wearing a football shirt … We always wear neutral clothes and shoes so that we could go out afterwards as well. [Hartlepool, aged 33 (MF)]

Similar temporary themes were noted of restaurants in the area of any given football ground. For instance in Darlington, participant Carl[1] recommends 'The Tapas Food Bar' as a venue for football fans before the match. He explains 'It gets in the match crowd because it has offers for fans on beer and food ... has football on the televisions and the staff know their football'. He concedes, 'If you went to the same place with your girlfriend at night, the atmosphere is totally different, you know – romantic. You wouldn't think it was the same place'. In Hartlepool, 'Jacksons Warf' is recommended by Luke[2] given that it has match-day offers on food and drink and 'welcomes all football fans to a friendly atmosphere filled with football memorabilia'. In Middlesbrough, Peter[3] mentions 'Walkabout sports bar for its atmosphere before the match', but like Carl he concedes that this establishment takes on a different persona on Saturday night 'to cater for night-clubbers'. In Newcastle, some restaurants that are not in the immediate vicinity of the ground were also noted to attract customers with 'match-day special offers':

> Ben: We sometimes go to Marco Polo's on the Quayside. If you guess the first goal scorer or whatever they will give you a refund after the match if you take back the receipt. [Newcastle, aged 30 (STH)]

Fans, like those above, are aware of the presence of commercial theming and are awake to the sense that this captures the imagination of, and creates excitement for, the passing football trade. Subsequently, they are attracted to establishments that become regular meeting spaces due to a themed connection and intimate level of service that helps to differentiate one experience from another. Moreover, fans are conscious that such service-based establishments (pubs, restaurants, bars) are not exclusively football themed, and yet, given that the theme need only last as long as the event itself (a short period of time before and after the live match), this was unproblematic for participants. The fact that restaurants or bars change themed ambience to suit a specific passing trade, even discriminating against the football crowd in the late evening by catering specifically for the Saturday night party theme (see Kirsty, above), or as a space for romantic couples (see Carl, above), does not seem to negatively affect consumer relations with football fans.

Theming is loose and fluid in this sense, and yet it upholds a schedule of change that is predictable, stable and therefore reliable enough for fans to depend on and internalise as an authentic part of match day practice. Thus, it seems that service-based establishments on the periphery of the football stadium can afford

---

1 Carl [Darlington, aged 23 (MF)].
2 Luke [Hartlepool, aged 21 (STH)].
3 Peter [Middlesbrough, aged 32 (STH)].

to remain flexible in their adoption of themed experiences. They can find comfort in the role of 'commercial omnivore', feeding off and responding to the themed needs of a plethora of potential customer types (including, but not exclusively featuring, the football fan). It is quite possible therefore, for service providers to be known and appreciated under the guise of different themed genres without conveying feelings of disruption or disloyalty to diverse customer profiles. Hence, those businesses that have developed in accordance with consumer society and the potential demands of match-day audiences, have in essence infiltrated and consequently altered the match-day experience by virtue of creating a variety of themed options for sports fans to consider:

> Rod: Well my routines have definitely changed over the years due to the amount of things available for us fans, you know … there's various promotions at bars, restaurants, you know, just nicer facilities really give you choice of things to do in the hours leading up to or after the game. It's a lot different now than it was when I was a kid. [Sunderland, aged 28 (STH)]

For the football club, theming takes on a different persona. Rather than competing for custom with other external leisure providers, differential match-day packages (internal to the club) are made available for the fan. Beyond the notion of simply buying a ticket to watch a game of football, fans have the option to choose from one of the more sophisticated, expensive and socially elevating executive packages. Martin explains:

> Martin: You've probably got three types of executive packages. You've got the box where they bring you your meal in and you've got your own bar and you have your own member of staff to assist you and all that bollocks. You've got the one where you can have your dinner and then go out to a posher seat, and then there's 'club 1892'[4] which is basically a step above the common man where you can go and stand in the nicer bar instead, without the excessive queuing of the concourse, get a free programme before the game. [Newcastle, aged 42 (STH)]

Market segmentation of this type (above) 'increases the inclination to consume' (Bryman 2004: 4) by creating exclusive packages that are themed specifically in order to sell the same experience (that is, the live match) at a premium rate. The pricing structure is marked out according to the exclusivity and prestige attributed to a specific themed experience. Prestige undoubtedly communicates a sense of economic and cultural capital which broadly infers the financial status and potential

---

4 Club 1892 refers to the use of an exclusive bar for those fans that pay a premium for a specific match-day package at Newcastle United. 1892 is the year that the club was officially founded.

cultural wealth that an agent may possess (Wacquant 2008). Furthermore, it is worth noting that those unable to afford 'high end' themed tickets nevertheless perceive this business strategy as desirable for the football club:

> Neil: The way I see it is that they've got more money than sense but if they are willing to spend it, it benefits the club and I'm all for that. [Sunderland, aged 19 (STH)]

Although Neil (and fans like him) cannot afford tickets with high price structures, it is not uncommon for fans to place the greater interests of the club beyond personal concerns (Giulianotti 2005). After all, the football club denotes what Beardsworth and Bryman (1999) would describe as a 'reflexive theme' in the sense that 'it' (the football club) consistently maintains popularity across time and space, based solely on the historical and cultural signs that it produces. Consequently, like parents looking out for the interests of a child, fans are aware of 'what is good for the club', and they too spend money accordingly in order to contribute to its welfare:

> Nats: I'm not a football fan I'm a Boro fan. I live and breathe the Boro and genuinely couldn't give a monkey's about any other football team … Red through and through. I pay my money every week for the boys. Come on the lads! [Middlesbrough, aged 24 (STH)]

In spite of the consistency of theming in some quarters of football (for example, relating to the football club as a reflexive theme) it was noted by participants that sub-themes such as football competitions and leagues are often re-branded for the sake of corporate advertisements and global marketing. Re-branding in this manner offers a clear market strategy that attempts to reposition and pair a product (for example, a football tournament) with a mutually beneficial and successful commercial sponsor. This strategy pursues a form of theming that has proven to develop brand awareness for both parties, given that they are often discussed interchangeably (Bryman 2004, Crawford 2004, Horne 2006). Moreover, from the perspective of the football fan, this late modern development brings with it an added suggestion of excitement that appeals to the contemporary football crowd:

> Carol: When I was a kid it was division 1–4. Now they've got more sexy titles to sell, they've been rebranded to make things seem more exciting. You know – the second division is now the Coca Cola Championship and the fourth is League

2.[5] It doesn't seem as bad when you say it like that ... A bit of glamour is good for us all! [Hartlepool, aged 43 (STH)]

Here, Carol is aware of the commercial significance of global theming, but in spite of this she, and many other participants, were tolerant of and spoke in complimentary fashion about this process as a model for bringing 'a bit of glamour' to proceedings. In a similar pose, participants also noted that football clubs were likely to re-brand football stadiums in order to create a more exciting and globally appealing themed brand:

Paul: 'The Riverside' and 'Stadium of Light' are clever marketing gimmicks aren't they? They sound more appealing for the television and the global audience. It's not the 'grim North' anymore, its names that are much more appealing to other potential fans, say in China or somewhere like that. [Middlesbrough, aged 53 (STH)]

Sunderland's move from Roker Park to 'The Stadium of Light' in 1997, and Middlesbrough's move from 'Ayresome Park' to 'The Riverside Stadium' (formerly known as the Cellnet and Later BT Cellnet Riverside Stadium until 2002 due to a themed sponsorship agreement with the telecommunications company) in 1995, are noted by Paul (above) as clear attempts to cast off local, depressed images that tend to be associated with the ex-industrial heart of Northern England, in order to create an image that would appeal to a global market of consumers. Instances like these are becoming common place in English football with cup competitions, leagues and stadium names open to commercial sponsorship. Of the twenty Barclays Premier League teams in the top tier of English football (season 2011–12), seven club stadiums now hold the name of their sponsor in the title[6] as they attempt to embed commercial enterprise into the cultural fabric of the football club. The latest club to adopt this strategy in November 2011 is Newcastle United. The stadium name was changed for the purpose of commercial theming from its founding name 'St. James Park', to 'The Sports Direct Arena', a deliberate move to market the

---

5 Coca Cola ended sponsorship with the Football League in 2009. *Npower* have been the new league sponsors since 2010.

6 The following Premier League stadiums (2011-2012 season) are named after sponsors: The Britannia Stadium (Stoke City) – Britannia Building Society; DW Stadium (Wigan) – DW Sports Fitness; Emirates Stadium (Arsenal) – Emirates Airlines; Etihad Stadium (Manchester City) – Etihad Airways; Liberty Stadium (Swansea) – Liberty Property PLC; The Sports Direct Arena (Newcastle) –Sport Direct.

business 'Sports Direct' to football's global audience.[7] Hence, whilst authors such as Duke (2002) speak of resistance from fans towards commercial theming of this type, it should be noted that resistance tends to be mild in nature as the process of commercial theming continues to gather momentum.

According to both Horne (2006) and Sandvoss (2003) television broadcasting is thought to be a catalyst for the adoption of this commercial strategy and the role that it plays in fusing or even confusing cultural and commercial genres. Rupert Murdoch's satellite television company News Corporation is noted by both authors as a pivotal player in the global vision of the Premier League in 1992. Consequently, Horne (2006: 50) reminds us of the depth of Murdoch's financial control over the sport:

> In the UK, News Corporation's Sky TV won an exclusive deal worth £304 million with the English Premier League in May 1992. By 1996 it controlled ninety per-cent of the revenues generated from subscription TV. It then secured a new five-year deal with the Premier League worth £670 million ... Murdoch's company have continued to acquire sports exclusives since then.

Despite clear financial control over sport and an overt themed programming schedule designed to fragment Premier League fixtures in order to enable mass audience viewing (including programmes such as 'Ford Super Sunday'; 'Monday Night Football'; 'Sky Sports News'; Gillette Soccer Saturday', etc.), Murdoch's business strategy for football was somewhat less intrusive than it had been for other sports. For instance, with reference to Murdoch's takeover of the Rugby Super League in 1996, Falcous (1998: 11) describes how a deliberate and revolutionary marketing strategy was employed by Murdoch in an attempt to make the game more attractive to a wider audience with the added incentive of de-localising or diluting local connections:

> Old team names typically made reference to local industry, places, land marks and historic team colours. Based firmly in the locality, these names have been replaced by anonymous, 'placeless' titles. Thus the Barrow club, formally known as the Shipbuilders have become the 'Braves', Whitehaven Colliers, the 'Warriors' and Castleford Glassblowers, the 'Tigers' and so on. Additionally, the traditional club crests have been replaced by more marketable logos that lack local connections.

---

7 On 9 October 2012, payday loan company Wonga.com became Newcastle United's main commercial sponsor and purchased the stadium naming rights. They subsequently announced that the St James' Park name would be restored as part of the deal.

Rather than implementing a strategy to de-localise football in a similar way, there has been little talk of such dramatic changes in Murdoch's strategy for football. In English football, after all, the 'local' is 'globally recognisable' and valued, not only by fans of the club as part of their cultural heritage, but also by those whose chief concern is the commercial running of any given football club. Accordingly, club owners, chairmen and management structures are conscious of the commercial benefits that are associated with the prestige of belonging to the elite group of English clubs that can boast status as the founders of the global game. As a consequence, English teams have their roots firmly implanted in the very essence of football culture, and this is extremely marketable. Furthermore, clubs such as Middlesbrough FC have recently taken the step to re-emphasise the tradition of the club. This was deemed necessary by the club chairman Steve Gibson in 2007, given that the club badge had previously displayed the relatively recent date '1986' to signify Middlesbrough's re-birth following liquidation. On 11 May 2007 the badge was re-launched to accommodate the club's date of inception '1876' for what some conceive to be 'branding reasons':

KD: Why did Middlesbrough change the badge in 2007?

Colin: What I heard was that the old badge gave the wrong impression to the foreign market type of thing. Like people in the Far East or whatever saw the date on the Boro badge as a poor relation to other teams. Coz it said 1986, people presumed that it didn't have much of a history and presumably the foreign market buy into the historical side of the game, otherwise why change it? [Middlesbrough, aged 53 (STH)]

In support of Colin's analysis the explanation offered by the football club to the readers of the Middlesbrough FC unofficial website 'Boro Mad', reiterates the importance of embracing the long and distinguished heritage of Middlesbrough FC. The chairman of the football club, Steve Gibson, wrote: 'The new badge will ensure that everyone in football will know exactly how far back Middlesbrough Football Club goes'. Chief Executive, Keith Lamb, continued on this vein suggesting that '... during our European travels we met clubs having nothing like our tradition ... they should have been looking up to us, knowing our distinguished heritage but they actually thought we were formed as a new club just twenty years ago'.[8] In other words, it seems as though

8 Quotes from both Steve Gibson (Chairman) and Keith Lamb (Chief Executive) of Middlesbrough FC were sited on the fans Unofficial Website 'Boro Mad' in November 2009. http://www.middlesbrough-mad.co.uk/news/loadnews. asp?cid=TMNW&id=338119

the strength of the commercial brand and the heritage of the club are closely aligned. Age inevitably brings providence and a rich history that is used here to sell perceptions of grandeur to a new European market.

In sum – theming has become standard practice for all manner of institutions, and specific football themes are used accordingly. From the pubs and restaurants that draw on the match-day theme, to football clubs, leagues, stadiums, television networks and advertisers, theming is used to attract custom and to improve global appeal. For the football fan, it offers desirable sites for social interaction and consumption in coordination with the object of fandom.

Hybrid Consumption and Football Fandom

Hybrid consumption refers to 'the general trend whereby the forms of consumption associated with different institutional spheres become interlocked with each other and thus become increasingly difficult to distinguish'. (Bryman 2004: 57)

Hybrid consumption is inextricably linked to the process of theming. In fact, the existence of hybrid consumption depends on the volume and density of themed consumption opportunities that are available in any one space. Take the match-day experience as a typical example:

Rhona: There's loads to do ... Common facilities, if you like, for the normal supporter are all set out in the concourse.[9] You've got the bookies [gambling shop] which is Ladbrokes. A number of bars and burger stands just like McDonalds [global fast food restaurant] but Newcastle United Catering. You've got bank machines, large screen TVs ... [Newcastle, aged 23 (STH)]

Similar to the style of US baseball parks that are known to include food courts, beer gardens, video arcades and other consumption elements (Ritzer and Stillman 2001) Rhona explains that watching the match is only part of the experience. She alludes to various goods and services that are brought together in the stadium, each vying for the attention of the fan. Furthermore, Rachael (below) likens this enhanced experience to other leisure services such as going to the cinema. She explains:

Rachael: Going to the match is great. To be honest it's just like going to the cinema or something ... you buy your ticket to enter and then browse around,

---

9 The term 'concourse' is used here to refer to a large open space within the football stadium where supporters can gather before, during, or after the game.

buying this and that. You know, you buy your refreshments, maybe get a programme which is like a preview of a film and as you are doing this you're part of the atmosphere surrounding the main event. [Sunderland, aged 28 (STH)]

The stadium experience is designed in such a way that the football audience, much like the cinematic audience, value, enjoy and desire the hybrid opportunities for consumption that are made available prior to the main event. Moreover and further removed from the match-day experience, the stadium also presents a site for hybrid consumption on any regular day.

Andy: There's stuff to do at St. James even when it's not match-day. There's the museum; the biggest Adidas store in the world which runs the length of the Gallowgate stand; and Shearer's Bar which is open all week, through the day as well as at night ... It's traditionally a 'sports bar', you've got tellys on all over the place and they do beam back some of the away games that are not televised elsewhere and you have to pay a couple of quid to get in. [Newcastle, aged 50 (MF)]

When describing 'Shearer's bar' (that is, a public house integrated within the walls of St. James' Park Stadium [opened in 2004]) Andy uses the term 'traditional sports bar'. This is worthy of note given that the concept of 'the sports bar' is itself a relatively recent commercial construction that has been used for marketing reasons as a hook to differentiate from other standardised pubs and bars (Bryman 2004, Kraszewski 2008). Thus, the sports bar reveals an explicit case of theming that this participant willingly consumes as an authentic form of fandom practice. Perhaps more significantly, it seems that participants are dependent on hybrid consumption opportunities in order to explain any aspect of practice. Take for instance, Roy's description of a typical match-day:

Roy: On the day of the match, typically, I get the papers to read with breakfast. Sometimes my Granddad brings around Friday night's Northern Echo as well ... I have a chat with him about the match and we watch Sky Sports ... I check out the internet ... log onto the club website and various other general sites like Sky News and the BBC, twitter and facebook[10] to join in banter ... If we're playing at home I meet my mates, then we get the bus to the ground.

KD: What do you do when you get there?

---

10 Created by Jack Dorsey (an American web designer and businessman), 'Twitter', is an online social networking and microblogging service that enables its users to send and read text messages of 140 characters, known as 'tweets'. Likewise 'Facebook' is a social networking service, owned and operated by Facebook INC. Mark Zuckerberg (co-founder) is chairman and chief executive.

Roy: I always get a programme and put my bets on. Two pints in the stadium, meet some others and hang out ... watch the dancing girls, Boro's answer to the Spice Girls [laughing] ... There's different entertainment all the time ... local kids playing five-a-side, the good old mascot, competitions to hit the cross bar, raffles, and tunes to get the crowd going ...

KD: What about half time?

Peter: At half time I get a meal deal. Pie and chips usually. We are well known for our balti pies. Maybe a coffee if it's cold [weather] ... Afterwards we either go home or to the pub to discuss key points. [Middlesbrough, aged 26 (STH)]

Here Roy makes explicit use of various modes of consumption to describe the match-day experience, acknowledging two sites for hybrid consumption. First, hybrid consumption occurs in the home – involving the delivery of newspapers and the consumption of themed television programmes and internet websites. Second, within the stadium vicinity – purchasing a drink; gambling; match-day programme; and a meal deal. Additionally the presence of pre-match entertainment in the form of dancing girls, club mascots, museums and sports shops, are akin to the American style of delivery which creates an atmosphere to encourage continued consumption (Duke 2002, Bryman 2004).

On this evidence I suggest that processes of theming and hybrid consumption play a significant and increasing role in the evolutionary process of football fandom. To be clear, I am not suggesting that fans are necessarily duped by the mechanics of Disneyisation, however, I do suggest that the design of the match-day space purposively creates an atmosphere conducive to consumer behaviour. In other words, the excitement of match-day sociability, when combined with hybrid consumption opportunities, converge to create a carnivalesque atmosphere capable of lulling consumers to drop their guard and perhaps spend more freely:

Charlene: Match-days are just good fun. I go with my dad and, like, it's the best mood I ever see him in all week, it's just a special atmosphere that does something to you. Like, you end up doing stuff that you wouldn't normally do.

KD: Like what?

Charlene: Well, like gambling, eating junk food, drinking Bovril and that. If I wasn't at the match I wouldn't do any of those things, and like, my dad is never that generous normally. [Newcastle, aged 21 (STH)]

As the examples above illustrate, the match-day experience displays all of the characteristics of a specialised shopping sphere designed to encourage spending but perhaps most significantly, customers appear to be grateful for this opportunity. Participant Keith,[11] for instance, recalls attending football thirty years ago and insists that he would 'be the first to complain if standards went backwards'. He continues, 'it's a privilege to step foot in the stadium we've got now … fans are well catered for … we've got nothing to complain about'. In this capacity, leisure services within the stadium offer a form of comfort that the football fan can rely on:

> Linda: I don't buy that much when I go to the game … Though, I do want opportunities to buy – say, good food or a coffee if I want one. I do expect a professional service, and I like the all the trimmings, like large screen TV's in the concourse, the club shop and that … I do like the feeling that modern stadiums offer – The buzz. It's not just the match that people like, but the choices that we have within the stadium – they are second to none and that is one major reason that I choose to spend my leisure time there. [Sunderland, aged 28 (STH)]

> KD: Would you stop going if certain services were taken away?

> Linda: Well, I can't say yes for certain, but I would have to seriously reconsider my position as a season ticket holder … Tickets are that expensive now that I expect a quality service … the club must continue to look after paying customers.

Whether fans choose to consume (economically speaking) or not, hybrid consumption opportunities are valued. Moreover, if removed, fans like Linda (above) suggest that they may reconsider their situation as season ticket holders in future. This position demonstrates an attitude that must please leisure proprietors. As Linda suggests, it seems that the desired reward for loyalty is that the club should 'look after the fan' by offering more opportunities to consume and spend money within the ground and beyond. In essence then, hybrid consumption opportunities have infiltrated and consequently altered the match-day experience by virtue of creating a variety of themed options for sports fans to consider. Once considered by potential customers, strategies for selling and maintaining customer satisfaction are employed by sales staff via the concept of emotional labour.

Performative Emotional Labour and Football Fandom

> Probably nothing epitomises or exemplifies emotional labour more than *the smile*. (Bryman 2004: 105)

---

11 Keith [Middlesbrough, aged 45 (MF)].

The term 'performative emotional labour' makes reference to the use and strategic promotion of emotion for the explicit purpose of enhancing customer satisfaction. With this, service providers ensure that employees are well drilled with various techniques such as smiling with authenticity and 'relaying only positive messages to potential customers' (Hochschild 1983: 4). When implemented correctly, the promotion of emotional labour can help to differentiate one customer experience from the next and encourage continued brand loyalty (Henkoff 1994). For the current participants, this concept resonates in diverse and often conflicting ways. First, fans have a confused view of who ought to embody emotional labour. Football players (as employees of the club) have a duty (according to participants) to display, in their performance, an emotional intensity which is admired and celebrated when it is embodied and disparaged when it is perceived to be lacking:

> Ian: Rob Purdie would be my favourite player. He's a one hundred percenter. He lays it all out there on the pitch and that's what the fans want to see. He wants to win and understands how important it is to the fans. [Darlington, aged 26 (MF)]

> Martin: I'll tell you what it is. That fucker couldn't care less [football player Michael Owen]. He's played about five games and he's picking up a big fucking cheque every week. Even when he plays he looks as though he doesn't want to … All of the fans out there would give their right arm to represent Newcastle. He's a waste of space. [Newcastle, aged 42 (STH)]

Attitudes towards football players Rob Purdie and Michael Owen respectively illustrate the desirable and undesirable characteristics that are attributed to sport workers based on emotional labour. However, in spite of this there is little evidence to suggest that such attitudes would impact on customer relations with the club in the sense that the Disneyisation thesis alludes to. For instance, whilst Bryman (2004: 105) suggests that 'as many as two thirds of customers stop purchasing a service or product due to dissatisfaction with an employee', it seems unlikely that football fans would curb spending habits due to the negative attitudes of star players. The likelihood is (given the global status of the player) that a disinterested and emotionally superfluous Michael Owen would (for example, financially speaking) benefit rather than harm business relations with fans.

> Kev: Big players draw in big crowds … Even though he's not playing well you can't buy his shirt [Michael Owen] anywhere. It's always sold out. [Newcastle, aged 23 (MF)]

Removed from the emotional intensity of players and in the purist sense of this concept, participants also refer to emotional labour as it is implicit within football club services such as executive packages, stadium tours and visits to the museum. Dougie[12] recalls that: 'the tour at the Stadium of Light was fantastic and well worth the entrance fee' on account that 'the guide was great with the bairns (children)'. In this instance the employee of the club was heavily praised for 'coming down to the level of the children' and 'making them feel the magic of the place'. Within scholarly literature this is something that Illouz (2009: 396) draws attention to when he discusses the presence of situational emotion. He explains that this phenomenon is often found in the consumption of tourist sites that are designed to produce intense experiences of nostalgia, authenticity, pride and excitement. Thus, in order to understand consumption, he suggests that it is important that we 'pay close attention to the ways in which emotions orient the activity of shopping as well as to the ways in which goods are packaged and designed'.

Similar praise and emotional connections were attributed to workers that exist beyond those official club services. For example, those working to sell official and unofficial programmes and even self-employed burger vendors that reside on the stadium periphery were praised for displays of emotional labour:

> Andrew: I get my burger from the same place each match-day. It's one of those dirt vans, but the bloke is good craic. We always have a craic about the match and that, and as soon as he sees me he gets my order prepared. He's a good bloke, he's like sound. [Sunderland, aged 44 (STH)]

The principles of emotional labour are omnipresent and readily apply to various products and services that are provided for the football fandom industry and yet it is important to note that additional elements of football fandom culture can further complicate this process. Here I am referring to a deeper sense of dissatisfaction that can be felt by fans towards the owners, shareholders and management structures within football clubs. For example, many interviewees felt unconvinced that the management structure shared an emotional commitment to the team or to the heritage of the football club more generally:

> Andy: What happened to 'the customer is always right'? Not in football they're not … I work for the Co-op and we would get sacked if we ran our business like the way football clubs do. Alienating your customers is generally not a smart move in business. [Newcastle, aged 50 (MF)]

Football supporters like Andy (above) voiced their discontent at the perceived lack of consideration awarded to fans by the owners of football clubs in spite of the fact that they (that is, as fans) consistently spend money at the club. This

---

12 Dougie [Sunderland, aged 37 (STH)].

can be a source of frustration for football fans, but when confronted with poor customer service, fans do not react in a typical consumer manner:

John: Boro's PR [public relations] is disastrous at times and they treat us [fans] like shit but we still go back and spend, spend, spend ... My mate is the biggest Boro fan; never missed a game home and away and he didn't get a ticket for the UEFA cup final. Disgrace. He was adamant that he would never step foot in the ground again.

KD: Did he stop going?

John: That's the thing, no. He can't stop! Boro is in his blood ... [Middlesbrough, aged 42 (MF)]

This illustrates an emotional differentiation between regular consumer practices and the consumption of football fandom. After all, as Lord Justice Taylor, in his final report on the Hillsborough Stadium disaster (cited in Mullin, Hardy and Sutton 2000: 28), points out, 'no one has their ashes scattered down the aisle of Tesco's' and hence, with Taylor, I argue that fans possess a genuine form of emotional labour that serves to encourage consumerist activity. Here, John (above) suggests that the gravitation towards consumption is likened to a form of compulsion based on emotional ties. This position is congruent with Illouz (2009: 388) who argues that it is vital that we consider emotion as a crucial component of consumption per se, and desire more specifically. He claims that 'consumption leans on an extraordinarily ruthless economic engine, but it simultaneously speaks to the softest crannies of our psyche'. Ben-Zeev (2000: 50) agrees with this contention, suggesting that even Bourdieu's conception of taste would benefit from a more explicit discussion of emotion. It may be appropriate then, to suggest that taste is not only influenced by classification schemes (for example, relating to one's social position) but also through intense feelings (for example, emotions) acquired and acted out through one's habitus, pre-understandings and practical consciousness. This position was supported by participant Tina:

Tina: I don't buy all the stuff that I have because I need it. I buy it because I want to show my support. My love for my team. That's why I do it. I always have and always will. [Middlesbrough, aged 25 (MF)]

Moreover, this connection has also been observed and put to use by marketing experts in order to encourage the sale of goods or services through the stimulation of both imagination and emotions. Take for example the following advertisement for Sky Sports 2009–2010 season. Rather than drawing on the promotional fixtures that will be shown or the celebrity athletes that will grace our television screens, the marketing focus was based on fans and their emotive connection to the club:

Visual Display Audio Dialogue

[Man jogging] Some of you may feel the way I do. [Female in football shirt] Some will feel more in love than the most beautiful story. [Male in field of rye] Some of you will travel great distances. [Male driving a car] Some of you have been doing this all your life. [Male in working overalls] Some of you may mutter the words ... If only ... [Female in working overalls] Too many times to be considered sensible. [Musician] Some of you may not be their all the time, but keep the faith nevertheless, [Picture of child] Some of you may take your sons and daughters. [Female in football shirt] And one day they'll take theirs. [Males at a BBQ] Some of you wear your heart on your sleeve. [Male in football shirt] Actually, you all do that. [Match-day crowd] Some of you are so proud because this is where you come from. [Crowd celebrating] Some of you will experience bursts of pure bliss. [Supporters travelling home] Some of you will never want the day to end. [Man jogging] Some of you will feel the way I do.

This advertisement evokes a range of emotions from feelings of love, commitment, loyalty, hope, irrationality and pride. Added to this were considerations of authenticity and tradition that were used to draw the customer closer to the televised product. With the following words (projected by the actor and Sheffield United supporter Sean Bean) the advertisement delivers a message of emotional congruence between the broadcasting company 'Sky Sports' and potential consumer fans:

Visual Display Audio Dialogue

[Sky Sports Logo] Football! We know how you feel about it, because we feel the same.

As Whannel (2009: 206) suggests, even in an environment where television channels have fragmented the mass audience, television sports (but particularly football) are one of the few forms that can still assemble exceptionally large television audiences. Consequently, emotional and cultural connections are brought together through this medium with intense commercial activity that commodifies the idea of the spectacle in advance of the live performance. In addition to this, celebrity football players, or local heroes such as Alan Shearer (former player and record goal scorer for Newcastle United), have also been used by media corporations for their appeal and emotional connection to a specific locality. For instance, Shearer has starred in a series of advertisements for the fast food restaurants 'McDonalds' and one participant in particular highlights the potential commercial business generated on the back of such promotions:

> KD: Do you think that advertising will make a difference to what people might buy?

> Dave: I would say yes. Yes it would, and I'll give you an example. Because of the God-like status of Shearer you get them all [fans] in Shearer's bar and when he did the McDonalds thing I'd like to bet one million percent that the match-day crowd were attracted to McDonalds even more so than normal. There were massive posters, billboards, life size cut outs – the wack! [Newcastle, aged 40 (STH)]

Whilst Wellman (2006) would question the moral responsibility of the sports star when using his/her image to promote a fast food restaurant, Bryman (2003) would suggest that this is evidence that even McDonalds have succumbed to the processes of Disneyisation and theming based on emotional connections. Similarly Moor (2008) indicates that affective attachments can be used by clubs and corporations as sources of added value to attach to their products, whilst other authors like Edensor and Millington (2008) reiterate the potential use of affective local ties for the marketing of football clubs per se. Emotive ties to and symbolic representations of the stadium have also been identified by Hughson (2004: 325) as important points of reference, or topophilic markers that are used beyond the immediate football audience. For instance, St. James' Park (home of Newcastle United) featured predominately in the promotional material that was used in the campaign for Newcastle upon Tyne to become 2008 European City of Culture. Hughson explains:

> Among this material was the video documentary *Beyond Imagination*, which concluded with Alan Shearer speaking from St. James' Park. Shearer declares his own background as a 'Geordie lad' … St. James' Park is the public site of Shearer's return home, and a point of communal gathering for other Geordies to engage in a carnivalesque expression of adoration for their local hero and local team.

For Hughson and Free (2006) evidence like this, helps to identify the club as a cultural commodity or a commercialised product whose meaning depends on fans (or residents of a particular locality) being able to see their own history as supporters embedded within the club. Consequently then, emotional performative labour can take a variety of forms within football fandom practice. First it works in the purist sense (in accordance with Bryman 2004) where employees or marketing experts are encouraged to provide a positive atmosphere (for example, by virtue of the implementation of a friendly and emotionally congruent persona) in order to improve the experience for customers, or else encourage customers to buy a product or service. Secondly, fans expect players to embody emotional labour and a certain emotional ethos which outwardly promotes a positive attitude and reflects their own emotional investment. Thirdly, because fans are part of the performance (and consider themselves as supporters as well as consumers) they too feel a duty to support the team via economic expenditure on club-related material and services.

Merchandising and Football Fandom

> Merchandising is a form of franchising in the sense that it is a mechanism for leveraging additional uses and value out of existing well known images. (Bryman 2004: 79)

Merchandising may not be exclusively related to the late modern period, however, Bryman contends that the variation and volume of products that are produced and sold by football clubs and governing bodies under the conditions of market exchange have increased significantly. Other scholars such as Giulianotti (1999), Horne (2006), and Crawford (2003, 2007) are in agreement with this position and suggest that even those agents that perceive authenticity to exist outside of the commercial sphere are catered for by museums, classic club shirts and videos/DVDs of old/classic games. Participants in the current sample provide evidence to support this assertion:

> Jimmy: I don't buy that much really, I don't think that's what football's about … Jackie Milburn, now he was a player. I bought a few DVDs last month of the 1950s team. Against Man City in the 1955 cup final Milburn scored in the first minute … Aye, those DVDs are great, it reminds me of what football used to be. [Newcastle, aged 55 (MF)]

Without exception, all interviewees were owners of football merchandise ranging from scarves, coats and hats, to coffee mugs, curtains and pillow cases, and in turn they describe such possessions as integral to fandom practice. Even those who initially refute the tag of 'merchandise owners' eventually succumbed to this conclusion:

> KD: Do you buy football related merchandise at all?

Tim: No. It's just not me. I mean, I've got all of the accessories, but they last for years, you know? The scarf, the hat, the gloves and the coat. I get the top [replica shirt] every other year. You've got to have those things as a fan, but you don't buy them all the time. [Pause] On reflection though, that's quite a lot isn't it? [Middlesbrough, aged 54 (MF)]

To illustrate how this dependable and sometimes unconscious relationship between fan and consumer goods continues to thrive as a feature of late modern fandom, a line of questioning regarding the origins of practice began to reveal the crucial role that commercial merchandise can play in one's early experiences and concomitant initiation into the practice:

Kelly: Even before I could talk my dad had got me a Newcastle baby bib, which said 'The best dribbler at St. James Park' and it went from there really. Every birthday or Christmas I always got Newcastle presents I think just to make sure that I was still a fan. [Newcastle, aged 25 (MF)]

Supplementary to those Disneyised marketing strategies that are used to sell a product or service, participants (like Kelly above), illustrate an accompanying process. Here I refer to the conscious acquisition of merchandise for the purpose of gift exchange. According to McCracken (1986: 78) the process of buying merchandise for others reveals the conscious presence of 'exchange rituals'. He explains that the gift giver chooses a particular offering because it possesses meaningful properties that he or she wishes to see transferred to the gift receiver. In other words, 'the giver' invites 'the receiver' to define themselves in its terms (for example, as a fan of the associated football club). According to Giddens (1984), situations like Kelly's (above), are best explained with reference to the enforcement of 'authoritative resources'. That is where, in this instance, the parent draws on a position of dominance to generate command over others. Accordingly, material goods are put to work through an expressive form of gift giving (infiltrated with symbolic properties) favourable to the will of the parent, and ultimately, to the encouragement of fandom behaviour in the child. Thus, removed from Bryman's assertion that 'merchandisers must tread carefully' not to upset or disillusion parents with 'excessive marketing of temporary goods' (2004: 100), the evidence in this instance indicates that agent's desire, use and rely on merchandise to satisfy a personal agenda:

Andrew: I've got two kids and yes, I think it is my duty to make supporters out of them.

KD: How do you do that then?

Andrew: I think it's about being enthusiastic about the team and showing how important it is to you … Me and my brothers and dad just buy them all the gear and all the novelties. My son is only six and his bedroom is covered in Sunderland wallpaper, curtains, bed sheets, cuddly toys, posters all that … His uncles always keep him up to date with latest gear and he loves it. [Sunderland, aged 44 (STH)]

It is clear that merchandise can be used as a coercive tool to stimulate an interest in the practice or to promote a continuation of kin tradition. This pattern then becomes a routine occurrence that is particularly acted out on birthdays, Christmas holidays, or to mark the beginning of the new football season as participant Stuart recollects:

Stuart: … Any presents that we got were generally football related. We were just football crazy really. Any new promotion: stickers, coins, magazines and that, we just had to have them … I just always wanted the next thing. That's what my little one is like now. Learned it off his dad probably. [West Ham, aged 45 (MF)]

Such reflexive accounts allow us to consider the possibility that one's desire for merchandise is a learned process that is passed down in an active and reciprocal manner from one generation to the next. Furthermore, there is evidence to suggest that desire to consume in this manner can bypass personal taste. Participant Wayne, for example, indicates that he dislikes the colour red but makes an exception for all Middlesbrough FC merchandise and Michael too infers that he is 'always first in the queue' to buy the replica shirt regardless of its personal appeal.[13] Moreover, when asked if he feels exploited by the extent of merchandising in respect to the changing designs of the replica shirt, Michael responded:

Michael: Not really. I'd be gutted that other teams were getting new designs while we got nowt to look forward to … We surely wouldn't want our teams to wear the same strip over again, that would just be dull … It adds a bit of spice to proceedings. We always chat about what the strip will look like, the new designs and that. It kicks off the season with a bit of excitement; everyone's like 'have you seen the new strip'? [Sunderland, aged 20 (MF)]

Likewise, whilst other participants were more sceptical of the rate that new strips are designed and sold to customers, they still sought to purchase the shirt.

Martin: Don't get me wrong I don't object to sales of the shirt, it's just when they change it too often that they bug me. For a while in about 1996 it went wild. There were about five different strips in the space of two years. For me, that was

---

13 Michael [Sunderland, aged 20 (MF)]; Wayne [Middlesbrough, aged 35 (MF)].

taking the piss ... Generally though, the way I see it is that buying the strip once per year is like paying your subs. [Newcastle United, aged 42 (STH)]

The reference to 'paying ones subs' (above) suggests feelings of duty to purchase based on emotive connections to the club and the concomitant outcome of effective marketing strategies featuring theming and hybrid consumption displays. The club shop is perhaps the most significant venue for merchandise displays of this type, often selling everyday household objects for a premium price:

Tim: ... items that are sold holding your team's identity [club badge] become desirable ... Like I've said, Middlesbrough wallpaper or bog roll is no better than Asda's own economy brand, but for a football fan it is worth the extra pounds shillings and pence ... Logic goes out the window for most fans. [Middlesbrough, aged 54 (MF)]

The attraction towards symbols of self and group identity (via merchandising) appears to be symptomatic of a learned response, ingrained into a habitus that places value on the purchase of products associated with the club badge. For instance, participant Kelly speaks of receiving gifts (as a child) from significant others and 'recognising the importance of the badge at an early age'. Similarly, Tim acknowledges his role as a parent to pass on the tradition of fandom by 'kitting out' his son 'with all the gear'. In support of this finding, Crawford (2004) suggests that despite the fluidity of late modern life, sports fans are likely to learn and replicate the norms of a particular habitus and Robson (2000: 169) too indicates that practical mastery of the practice of fandom becomes embedded into the very perceptions and dispositions of fans to such an extent that actions and thoughts are simply known in practice as 'the way things are done'. This, of course, can have positive implications for service providers:

Rebecca: If they played in a black and white bin bag I'd buy it for forty quid [pounds]. [Newcastle, aged 24 (MF)]

Perhaps then, the most significant outcome to arise as a by-product of Disneyised marketing procedures is the self-regulating relationship that has developed between the fan and the brand logo. In the end the shirt, the pencil case, the poster and the scarf resemble much more than the physical materials that are used to produce the item. The symbolic presence of the team colours and badge combine with one-another to transform a utilitarian but lifeless item into a symbol of self and group identity that harbours an emotional connection. Hence, participants were evidenced to infuse symbolic meaning onto material items, putting those resources to use as tools via the construction of identity:

Matty: I remember when I first moved in with the wife. She ironed a bloody big 'V' on the thing and she just, like, laughed sort of thing. I tried to make her understand. I said it's important to me, it's who I am, it's my heritage. She was like 'Don't be so dramatic it's only a shirt'. I said 'it's not 'only a bloody shirt!' It's like she thought it was only a fashion item or something. [Middlesbrough, aged 32 (STH]

In this instance (above) the shirt resembles much more than the physical materials that are used to produce an inanimate garment. The symbolic presence of the team colours and more importantly, the team badge, combine with one another to transform a utilitarian but lifeless shirt into a symbol of self and group identity that harbours an emotional connection. However, whilst this is true the level of emotional connection to material objects that are emblazoned with the club badge can vary:

Carol: I think definitely the shirt is the most important thing that you can buy. I mean you watch the game in your shirt and when your team score you kiss the badge, it just means so much. But things like my piggy bank [club branded money box] are not so important and don't have any deep meanings to me or anything like that. [Hartlepool aged 43 (STH)]

Nevertheless, Willis (1990: 27) has coined such affective attachments to commodities of mass culture as 'grounded aesthetics'. With this he suggests that capitalist culture has (almost unwittingly) provided for agents tools for further symbolic expression. Hence, 'commerce and consumption' he explains, 'have helped to release an explosion of everyday symbolic life and activity'. An important point to take from Willis is that football memorabilia, paraphernalia, ephemera and associated services are not simple commodities in the economic sense. The shirt, posters, scarves and other forms of merchandise are taken at the point of sale, appropriated, fused with meaning at personal and cultural levels and embodied within processes of everyday existence. Therefore purchasing is an aspect of financial, emotional and symbolic support or investment rather than a one dimensional form of commodity fetishism. Participant, Lee, provides the example in this instance:

Lee: When I went to the UEFA Cup final I kept, like, loads of tokens of memory. I've got official stuff like the programme, and other stuff like bus tickets, advertisements, beers mats all that stuff. Along with the actual ticket and a photograph of the lads that I went with, I got it framed and it's on my wall in the front room. It means quite a lot to me really. It's memories of a great adventure watching my team play; part of my history; priceless really. [Middlesbrough, aged 24 (STH)]

The adventure, as Lee describes it, has become inseparable from those mundane, functional commodities such as the match ticket and even the bus ticket that was later used to signify his arrival at the game (thus adding to the authenticity of the fan narrative). Commodities have a story to tell, both in pure commodity form (what Willis 2000 calls 'bearer form') and in terms of cultural usefulness. In other words, the meanings that are cast upon commodities are always constrained to an extent (based on the production process) and yet the necessity to stimulate communication eventually results in the implementation of grounded aesthetics.

Take the football shirt as an example, a garment that was put to use in various guises beyond the original intention of the manufacturers. Interviewees made explicit the processes via which goods were put to work in creative ways by loosening those commodities from their origins. Amongst other uses, the shirt was framed and mounted on the wall as art, it became a car seat cover, and it was even physically altered to undergo transformation into a feminine style as the following participants explain:

Luke: I don't wear the shirt much but I do have a framed shirt on my wall. It looks tidy (good). I use it as wall art ... A number of my mates have done it now. [Hartlepool, aged 21 (STH)]

Ian: Football fans are inventive with the merchandise available. I mean I use the Darlo shirt as a car seat cover. See, I work all over the North East so this way everyone knows who I support. [Darlington, aged 26 (MF)]

Sarah: When I first started going to the match there was nothing for girls. So when a girl bought a shirt she had the choice of buying the man's or the boy's. So, like it was totally unsuitable for women ... What we did was we tied our shirts up, or cut into them a bit, so they had either a plunging neck line or they just fit a little better ... [Newcastle, aged 42 (MF)]

Whilst the first two examples invoke clear ideas of identity promotion using external sites (that is, other than the body as intended) to display the shirt, the third illustrates how some of our female fans have altered the shirt from its original appearance at the point of sale, in order to create a more feminine look. It is worth noting that for those female participants represented in this sample, the consumption of signifying merchandise was deemed particularly important:

Wanda: As a woman I'd say that you need to prove that you are more of a fan, so you need to display it through clothes and all that. [Darlington, aged 21 (STH)]

Female fans like Wanda seemed aware (to a heightened extent) of the public gaze and concomitantly felt the need to display fandom identity via the consumption of merchandise. Likewise, Nicola speaks of the pressure that female fans feel to buy the latest designs:

> Nicola: I must admit I do feel pressured into buying because people will say like, 'I thought you were a true fan, why don't you have the latest shirt'? Like they're questioning your status as a supporter or something. [Newcastle, aged 27 (MF)]

In addition to the purchase of mass produced commodities, five female participants had tattoos of the club badge permanently sketched onto their bodies. On questioning, it was clear that this act of consumption and appropriation was ultimately used to demonstrate a certain dedication to the cause, or a sign of commitment that would rival any criticism regarding authenticity:

> Kelly: What more can I do than get the club engraved on my skin. It has become part of me and I think a tattoo signifies this in a way that nothing else could. It's permanent like my support, it's always going to be with me and I'm never going to get fed up of it. [Newcastle, aged 25 (MF)]

Tattooing, like other forms of consumption, is used by fans in creative ways to express or communicate identity and authenticity. To reiterate the thoughts of Bourdieu (1984), acts of consumption double as avenues for communication, and while communication (of the type above) may resonate primarily at an individual level, it is nevertheless influenced by histories, traditions, cultures and new opportunities for interaction. Thus, on reflection, it is clear that the reflexive habitus of late modern football fandom is infiltrated not only with cultural norms related loosely to football and specifically to kin group interpretations of fandom (see Chapter 4), but also to a commercial dynasty that has matured with the game and with those social agents devoted to it. As Lash and Urry (1994: 64) explain, in late modern life, 'the economy is increasingly culturally inflected and ... culture is more and more economically inflected'. Consequently the 'boundaries between the two are becoming ever more blurred'. They have become blurred via the integration of corporate marketing schemes, hybrid consumption opportunities, and the seemingly authentic presence of themed merchandise for sale. But whilst the analysis of the consumption and appropriation of material commodities can be valuable in the quest to detail the everyday consumption experiences of football fandom, it is worth noting that 'most of the time' fans do not consider themselves to be consuming per se (Warde 2005). Therefore, any discussion of consumption often falls short of those experiential modes that arguably make up the bulk of football fandom culture. With this in mind, it is to those experiential aspects of consumption and wider practice that I now turn in Chapter 6 when I deal more explicitly with fandom and routinisation.

Chapter 6
The Routinisation of Football Consumption in Late Modern Life

> ... it is commonly taken for granted amongst social analysts that the more abstract rules – e.g., codified laws – are the most influential in the structuring of social activity. I would propose, however, that many seemingly trivial procedures followed in daily life have a more profound influence upon the generality of social conduct. (Giddens, 1984: 22)

In this chapter I acknowledge routine processes of consumption that are frequently overlooked by academics and social agents alike. It is important to remember that routine acts of consumption are not simply repetitive forms of behaviour that are 'carried out mindlessly and without significance' (Giddens 1984: 86 and above quote). On the contrary, routines have a profound influence on the strength and direction of social conduct and it is on those grounds that I seek to explore the routinisation of football consumption in late modern life. Consequently, this chapter is segmented into three parts. It begins by discussing the underpinning motivations behind the routine consumption activities of football fans with specific links to emotional ties and feelings of security. As a second feature it considers the link between routine, sociability and cultural capital, and finally, the work moves to examine sites for the evolution of routine consumption. With respect to the latter point, it makes particular reference to the integration of emerging consumer activities, such as watching football in the pub and the use of new internet technology. Each mode is discussed in relation to the manner that it has emerged to become part of new routines, with details about how they are experienced and consumed illustrated throughout. I begin, however, by recalling a quote from Giddens (1984: 60) which captures the essence of this chapter. He states:

> An examination of routinisation, I shall claim, provides us with a master key to explicating the characteristic forms of relations between the basic security system on the one hand, and the reflexively constituted processes inherent in the episodic character of encounters on the other.

Giddens argues that routine fulfils an important, if not understated, role in the understanding of social action. It provides a sense of security for practicing agents, whilst simultaneously but subtly introducing change to practice over time through social interactions. This may seem paradoxical, yet 'routine' and 'change' are part of the same process. Giddens contends that it is through social interactions that agents maintain feelings of security and consequently reproduce the conditions for continued practice. In essence, however, short term routines, he explains, can only offer a facade of continuity, given that over time agents interact with diverse groups of people and across institutions that are also involved in organic process's of transformation. As such, the study of routine can reveal both the short term maintenance of habitus, capital and ontological security on one hand and the subtle but long term evolution of football fandom practice on the other. This chapter aims to demonstrate this process via the experiences of football fans.

Routine Consumption, Security and Emotional Ties

It was common for participants in this sample to report a sense of security gleaned from the routine consumption of live football. Whilst some fans were regular stadium attenders, they often struggled to explain why they regularly pay an over-inflated ticket price (irrespective of team performance or league position) for an ultimately disappointing act of consumption:

> Craig: Even when they're playing crap I still come back. I still pay my money every season … The first game that I missed at the Riverside, it was a surreal feeling. I should have been there … I always end up going back. My dad's the same. He's been threatening never to return for twenty-five years but you can't turn your back. [Middlesbrough, aged 27 (STH)].

For Craig and his father, satisfaction with team performance is irrelevant to the repeat consumer action of attending the match. Poor performance can lead to dissatisfaction manifest within verbal threats to 'never return to watch another match', but this rarely materialises in reality. The threat 'never to return' was often overshadowed by the surreal feeling associated with missing a game or breaking routine – as Martin explains:

> Martin: The first time I wasn't at the match on a Saturday when I should have been, the overriding emotion was 'fuckin hell', I felt lost. I just felt anxious. I know it sounds stupid but that's just what I felt. [Newcastle, aged 42 (STH)].

For Martin, the routine consumption of live football is closely associated with feelings of security. This is illustrated (above) when habitual and long-standing routines (that is, components of habitus) are compromised and anxiety ensues.

Similarly Banyard and Shevlin (2001) have indicated that performance-related disasters such as relegation from any particular league may result in high levels of psychological distress on account of the emotional investment and the consequential breakdown of routine. There is no direct evidence of this in the current sample per se (most likely due to the fact that interviews were carried out in the early to mid-season when relegation was a distant thought) but a number of participants had begun to acknowledge the possibility of relegation and the potential heartache that this would cause:

Kelly: It's not looking good for us at the minute and I'll be gutted if we go down.

KD: What would be the most upsetting aspect of relegation?

I don't know. It'll be embarrassing for a start, but probably the fact that we've been playing Man U, Arsenal and Chelsea every week for the past ten year, and like, if we get relegated it's like Blackpool ... We won't be on the telly much either so it will, like, totally mess up my viewing schedule. I just hope we can stay clear of the bottom three ... I know some people that will just be totally distraught. [Newcastle, aged 25 (MF)]

Feelings of embarrassment can again be linked to an emotional investment, not only in relation to 'team', but 'location' too. Participants wanted others to recognise the pride that they had invested in locality, and football stadiums were frequently used as a resource to signify this common bond:

Jimmy: I don't get there much but St. James' Park is like the centre of a community. Like a cathedral or something ... the football club is a place that most people can associate with and meet others ... It's a centre, a nucleus if you like where people go to gather ... If there's one thing I can't stand, it's when the mackems[1] get a chance to criticise the team and stadium. I think everybody is defensive about where we live and our identity is caught up in the football club. [Newcastle, aged 55 (MF)]

The football stadium, in the words of this participant, can be likened to the hub of a community or a central reference point for the consumption of football fandom. It is a secure space of symbolic importance from which to recall and remind oneself of the historical underpinnings of fandom practice. To paraphrase Bourdieu (1990: 57), it is likely that the stadium will appropriate the fan, just like 'property appropriates its owner, embodying itself in the form of a structure generating practices perfectly conforming with its

---

1 Jimmy uses the term 'Mackems' to make reference to Sunderland AFC supporters.

logics and demands'. Accepting this reason, the fan then consumes '... all the corresponding privileges and obligations ... providing quite real effects ... in belief'. Jack (below), in response to a rumour regarding a potential name change for the Newcastle United Stadium St. James' Park, typifies this point:

> Jack: What Ashley [Owner of Newcastle United at the time of interview] has got to remember is that St. James' Park isn't his. It belongs to all of us and it belonged to our fathers and their fathers before them. It belongs to the supporters and he's got to remember that. It's ours and he can't change the name without our support. [Newcastle, aged 27 (STH)]

As well as feeling ownership over the football stadium (and other symbolic properties such as the club badge) fans were also shown to consume the stadium in other ways. To briefly explain how this is so, it is worth introducing Soja's (1989, 1996, 2000) concept of 'city space'. Soja argues that city space (in this case, the football stadium) can be consumed at three levels (first, second and third space) with the initial two particularly insightful in the current context. 'First space', he explains, is associated with the logic of the Chicago school which directly connects space to social structure. Consequently, football stadiums are thought of as ideal sites for hybrid consumption (see Chapter 5). Furthermore, they are a tourist attraction for other fans to visit and therefore they become a form of cultural and material consumption per se:

> Darren: Everyone knows St. James! St. James' Park is one of the most famous stadiums in the world. People visit Newcastle just to say that they've been to St. James. There's almost always a full away support allocation because fans of football in general want to set foot in the stadium ... I'd go as far as saying it's a tourist site of national heritage. [Newcastle, aged 45 (MF)]

Whilst the football stadium undoubtedly provides a site for consumption at the level of first space, Darren (above) describes this landmark as a culturally reflective site of national heritage. This coincides with the concept of 'second space', revealing the routine mental reflection and emotional investment associated with urban features. Thus, the mental image linked with the stadium is enough to stimulate affective feelings that live on in fan consciousness irrespective of attendance at the venue. Willis (2000: 58) too provides support for this contention, and using the example of Manchester United fans who will never visit Old Trafford, he explains: 'meanings can carry from the far corners of the earth as easy as they can from around the corner'; a situation which participant, Bill can relate to:

> Bill: Obviously I'm a big Sunderland fan, but, as yet, I've not been to the Stadium of Light because I work away a lot ... I don't feel any less of a fan for it, no

… When I watch the match live on Sky Sports and see the supporters and the stadium and that; or even when I listen to the radio coming live from the ground – I still feel connected and immensely proud. [Sunderland, aged 34 (MF)]

Accordingly, Bill consumes the football stadium not through physical attendance, but by drawing on routine mental reflection of the physical reality of urban features (Kirchberg 2007: 124). In the spirit that Soja describes, this participant creates 'mental maps' that inevitably relate to longstanding, routine emotional connections. Comparisons can also be made here with Tuan's (1974) concept 'topophilia', a notion that is used predominately to explain the deep affection that people have towards particular social spaces, and furthermore, Bale (1993) has previously used this concept to make clear the affective dimensions associated with fans and sports grounds. However, it is worth noting that some scholars contest this notion in light of the contemporary advances to football culture in Europe. Sandvoss (2003) for instance, can see merit in the topophilic concept, but not for contemporary football fans. He suggests that football grounds are becoming placeless institutions that are devoid of any unique characteristics and as such they are thought less likely to evoke mass feelings of tophopillia, community, or belonging beyond projections of self. Nevertheless, in the current context, participants wholly represent the former position, holding specific affection towards the stadium of their supported team:

Lisa: It doesn't get full but *we love it*. It's just magic. [Darlington, aged 20 (STH)]

Laura: When you see the ground you get goose pimples. That's when you know you're going to the match. It's a special place. [Hartlepool, aged 20 (STH)]

'Mental maps' of the football stadium were recalled via personal experiences (in those instances above) and were explained, not only in terms of the physical surroundings, but by the sense of emotion that those physical surroundings exude. Additionally, the club and its physical landmarks were used to conceptualise something more than individual emotion. It was also used to relay visions of an imagined community of likeminded fans:

Jacko: It is Newcastle! You just couldn't imagine Newcastle without Newcastle United. When the club are riding high the city is buoyant … It is the bedrock of our city, it's a constant in our lives … [Newcastle, aged 28 (MF)]

The routine connection to the football club and its physical landmarks is only one means through which ontological security is maintained. In most instances sociability was a key driving force for routine practice; thus, in the following section I elaborate on the role of sociability (with particular reference to 'football chat') as a means for capital acquisition and the satisfaction of ontological security.

Football Chat and Sociability in the Pursuit of Capital

> Matty: It's all about getting together with my mates, that's what the routine is all about. That's what football has always been to me. Football is the glue that holds all my mates together … Without it, I doubt if we'd bother getting together. [Middlesbrough, aged 32 (STH)]

'Football chat' is a component part of football fandom that requires the routine acquisition and dissemination of football related knowledge. As such, it is not a passive activity. It involves, the active pursuit of mediated consumer sources such as national and local newspapers; news channels; national media internet sites; club websites; unofficial fandom and fanzine websites; message boards and social networking sites for the purpose of sociability:

> Kate: … being a fan definitely entails a responsibility of keeping in vogue with the latest movements of your club and beyond. [Middlesbrough, aged 18 (MF)]

> KD: How do you do that then?

> Kate: By any means possible to be honest. For me, I suppose the club website is my starting point or the paper (newspaper), but there's obviously TV and radio as well … I just keep my eyes and ears open … Oh, there's always discussions on Facebook as well …

Regardless of the mode of consumption and the necessary diligence required to consume information, agents are ultimately rewarded with cultural capital and a form of discursive stability when talking with others. Dougie[2] clarifies: 'I'm not a fantastic small talking person, but if people do want to talk with me, then footie is the obvious choice. It's comfortable for me. I'm totally at ease talking football'. He explains (in the manner that Giddens 1984 describes) that routine chat is linked to the minimising of unconscious sources of anxiety by providing agents (like Dougie) with a social buffer or a conversational escape route that is implemented when addressing other males in unfamiliar settings. Others too made similar points:

---

2 Dougie:[Sunderland, aged 37 (STH)].

Keith: Say I went up the brother in-law's or like say you're at a party and the two women get talking and you're stuck with the bloke, well you just make conversation talking about football to be honest. [Middlesbrough, aged 45 (MF)]

Here, both participants (Dougie and Keith) exemplify the wide ranging use of 'football chat' particularly in situations of discomfort (for example, being introduced to others for the first time). They acknowledge the potential of football as a socialising tool and as a safe, stable, discursive topic that can help agents to integrate socially. Yet, notwithstanding the capacity to aid with social inclusion, football chat was noted by males as a sign of normality and consequently, as a measure of masculinity:

Craig: It's a tool init? It's a tool to get involved in conversations. If someone can't talk about football in a group then that person basically gets sidelined. What you'll then find is that he doesn't drink beer ... It's a generalisation on a massive scale but I do find that, lads that don't like football [pause] there's something odd about them. [Middlesbrough, aged 27 (STH)]

In the instance above, consuming football as a discussion topic is placed alongside other typical 'manly' consumer activities such as 'drinking beer' and moreover, any deviation from this masculine standard is explained away as misguided and ultimately 'odd'. Such instances suggest similarities with participant Dougie's earlier discussion of childhood fandom. To recap, Dougie suggests that 'football is like a social badge' for young males and Craig (above) indicates that such attitudes do indeed carry through to adulthood as a component of one's masculine habitus and as part of the endless search for enhanced capital amongst peers. Concurrently, whilst the situation was clear for males (that is to say football chat is equal to increased cultural capital), the same could not be said of females. Female fans reported that they found it strange when peers did not share their passion for football, but it was they who tended to feel marginalised by female peers:

Holly: I have to try and completely avoid the subject! Especially if I'm with the girls, I mention it and they're 'just like shut the fuck up Holly'. I know those who I can talk with and those that I can't. [Hartlepool, aged 22 (MF)]

As evidenced here, there appears to be a gender difference, not necessarily in relation to the consumption of information, but in relation to everyday discursive practice. On one hand (only in relation to males) routine football chat can be used to root out those of questionable character – with football knowledge advancing cultural capital, or used as a benchmark for social acceptance. On the other hand, female fans routinely consume and discuss football, but they are conscious of when to apply knowledge in conversation. They do not appear to have the ease of exchange enjoyed by male counterparts and as portrayed earlier in Chapter 4, many female fans have referred to the difficulty of portraying 'authenticity'. Of course, this poses further questions in relation to the extent that reflexivity is apparent in late modern life and it is on this point that Adkins (2002) challenges the assumption that reflexivity is always transforming. She explains that reflexivity is forever related to normative values of any given time and space, including gender distinctions. Craib (1992: 150) agrees with this contention, arguing that whilst social agents are indeed reflexive beings; 'some of the time we find ourselves incapable of instituting changes'. This is reflected in Kirsty's understanding of female fandom.

> Kirsty: Scepticism of female fans is only to be expected. At the end of the day I'm a girl involved in a typical manly activity … Things are changing definitely, but in the mean time I can't change the fact that I'm a girl, so I have to live with any scepticism. I don't cry about it. That would be girly [laughing]. Like I say, it's to be expected. [Middlesbrough, aged 33 (STH)]

Kirsty's realisation of how the practice of football fandom works indicates that she is aware of a lack of influence or capital on account of gender. However, taken in this spirit and embraced for what it is, the ontological security of the subject is not breached to an alarming extent. The acknowledgement that things are getting better for female fans, coupled with the understanding that football is culturally positioned as a typical masculine sport, is enough to pacify the subject. After all, Kirsty explains that expectations of acceptance were already low, but improving. In Bourdieuian terms, this situation resembles one of misrecognition, that is 'an alienated cognition that looks at the world through categories that the world imposes, and apprehends the social world as the natural world' (Bourdieu 1990: 141). Hence, given Kirsty's acceptance of a negative gender order, it seems that she is subjected to a form of 'symbolic violence' that is exercised upon her with complicity (Bourdieu and Wacquant 1992: 194-5). It appears, then, that agents like Kirsty are limited in their social mobility aspirations within football cultures as they acknowledge the status-quo as the natural order of things (Webb et al. 2002).

Implications of Football Chat: Consuming 'Social Banter'

Beyond gender discrepancies relating to the consumption of knowledge and the acquisition of cultural capital, all participants enjoyed what was often described as 'banter'. Accepted in the terms that participant Rachael (below) describes, this concept involves using humour at the expense of opposing fans but paradoxically, it also involves a sense of self-deprecation:

Rachael: … It's being able to take the micky out of you and who you support, whether it be Sunderland, Middlesbrough or Newcastle. You know, they just take the micky. You 'rib' them [make fun] because they're a Geordie or they rib you because you're a Mackem. It's just the way that everybody gets along. It is a very big part of social life. [Sunderland, aged 28 (STH)]

By accepting the role as the 'ribber' and equally accepting that one is likely to be 'ribbed' by others, fans engage in a mutually accepted light-hearted form of dark humour where stereotypes of otherness are commonly and often routinely used for comic effect:

Tina: I love the banter. It is absolutely ridiculous stuff, but it's all good fun. You've got the sheep shaggers (Derby),[3] 'The Monkey Hangers' (Hartlepool),[4] 'The Smogs' (Middlesbrough)[5] on account of the chemical industry and, like, Liverpool slums, or car thieves.[6] It's totally unfair, but it's fun. [Middlesbrough, aged 19 (MF)].

A blend of self-enhancing and self-deprecating humour allows all to demonstrate their allegiance to a team whilst also indicating a level of approachability and friendliness (Martin, Puhlic-Doris, Larsen, Gray and Weir 2003). This blend enables fans to critique without producing negative interpersonal effects and in fact, it is more likely that relations with others will improve as a result of shared banter (Grugulis 2002). In agreement Morreall (1991) indicates that humour (used between fans) has a positive effect on socialisation processes, and given the temporal nature of success (for example, relative team success from one week to the next) shared laughter has the potential to bond agents together in the midst of adversity. Mutual humour of this type is an expected and stable aspect of social life that contributes to the ontological security of football fans:

Stacey: … win, lose or draw I take it on the chin. I know what to expect if we lose and I know what to dish out if we win … It's *comforting* and friendly. There's nothing remotely sinister about it. [Sunderland, aged 29 (MF)]

---

3 Nickname is on account of the club symbol 'The Ram'.

4 Nickname refers to a historic incident when the people of Hartlepool enforced capital punishment on a monkey in the town square (believing it to be a French spy).

5 Nickname is on account of the scale of industry in Middlesbrough.

6 Nicknames are based on stereotypical portrayal of Liverpool as a city for the underclass.

The predictability of banter as a result of the consumption of recent football knowledge is a comforting prospect for Stacey and whilst banter can occur in any social space, participants were particularly vocal and enthusiastic about the consumption of banter within the work environment:

> Colin: Coming into work with the boss being a scouser, me and Richie being Boro fans and Matt being a Leeds fan it's the first bit of banter we have ... I often walk in to work with a smile on my face just waiting to see Mark 'the scouse'. [Middlesbrough, aged 53 (STH)]

Colin clearly relishes the thought of engaging in banter and enjoys the anticipation of the possible reactions that his derogatory comments might cause. He was not alone with these thoughts, and as both Keith and Nicola (below) explain, in order to collect the desirable information that will form one's comic weaponry, fans must first scour a variety of consumer sources:

> Keith: If Soccer Saturday's on [Sky Sports News Programme] or I'm listening to the radio, I don't just look out for the Boro score, I look out for the results of my work mates as well so I can talk about it on Monday morning. [Middlesbrough, aged 45 (MF)]

> Nicola: TV, radio, internet, newspapers, and general gossip. I get my information from all over the place and when my friends' teams get beat I do take some pleasure in that – Definitely! It gives me a warm glow and I register it as ammunition for when I get back to work. [Newcastle, aged 27 (MF)].

Looking out for one another's results becomes a routine, ritualistic process of knowledge consumption. The aim of this routine practice is to ensure that agents have the potential, not only to remain within any given conversation, but also to instigate football chat with friends, colleagues, acquaintances and strangers. It seems that football fans must constantly improve or renew knowledge in order to bolster cultural capital. Moreover, for comic effect, those sought-after details can be trashy and trivial:

> Andrew: I make it my business to find out any scrap of slanderous information that I can use. Whether it's the misspelling of the word 'Boycott' by thick Geordies or like the latest jokes about Joe Kinnear [temporary manager of Newcastle United at the time of interview], whatever comes your way. [Sunderland, aged 44 (STH)]

For others, whilst humour clearly plays an important role, football and routine football chat or banter has and continues to provide life stability at a more sobering level:

Noel: Loads of stuff has gone on for me over the years but football has always been there for me … Did the usual, got married, had kids. Kids grew up and moved on with their own lives. The wife left a while back. All of those things have been difficult to deal with, particularly the divorce, but football's been good to me. It is my social life really. It's how I meet people; it's what I talk about and we have some fantastic banter. [Middlesbrough, aged 55 (MF)].

The routine consumption and dissemination of football chat/banter can be useful to fans in a plethora of ways and yet all experiences relate to the maintenance of security and the pursuit of capital. In relation to security, participants research and discuss football because they have always acted in this way – living out a learned practice that has historical and cultural connections. Secondly, participants are aware of the prestige that football knowledge can bring amongst peers. This encourages the active search for information in the endless pursuit of capital.

The Emergence of Consumption Routines: 'The Pub'

So far, this chapter has discussed, with illustrations, those underpinning motives that sustain routine consumption practice. What remains unclear, at this point, is the manner via which new consumption routines can begin and ultimately embed themselves in the practice of late modern fandom. Unveiling this process supports the contention that authenticity and tradition are ultimately time phased and temporary concepts that slowly transform in line with new consumption opportunities. These transformations in practice are, it is thought, inevitably associated with technological changes and allied commercial advances that have taken root in late modern society. However, more research is needed to investigate exactly how such technological changes have been integrated into the lives of fans and to explain how they contribute to greater freedom through forms of sociability and outlets for emotional expression (Cashmore 2000, Moor 2007). In order to address the issues raised above, the following draws attention to the new, but established, practice of viewing live football in 'the pub'; an institution renowned for its connection to football:

The pub has been a place in which to read about football, to talk about football, and to meet with friends before going to a live match. The pub provides a place where the male holy trinity of alcohol, football and male bonding come together. (Weed 2007: 400)

The pub and sport have always maintained a relationship of one form or another. Even before the industrial revolution Vamplew (1988: 26) indicates that the pub could be relied on as a stable space for recreation and the publican, as a supporter of organised entertainment. With a long and established history, the pub has fulfilled multiple consumer related purposes. It has taken the role of a shop, a bookmaker, and a place for working girls, musicians and magicians to practice their trade. Moreover, publicans have shown their hand as patrons for prize fights, cockfights, animal baiting and football competitions. Collins and Vamplew (2000: 2) explain this historical relationship:

> Certainly by the sixteenth century, and probably much earlier, the ale house was closely associated in the public mind with sport, as landlords found that the space adjoining their property could be utilised to promote sport events that would attract crowds. The yards, greens and grounds of the drinking place provided the spaces in which sports as diverse as skittles, quoits, bowls, boxing, wrestling, tennis, foot-racing, cricket and any number of games featuring animals could be staged. In order to stage the events ... the publican became the promoter of sports, arranging matches and providing prize money, as well as being the book maker ... there was money to be made.

As the authors suggest, the pub has become a timeless supporter of various consumer activities and this, according to Holt (1990: 63), explains its enduring institutional success. He suggests that 'the staying power of the ale house' ought to be attributed to its chameleon-like ability to adapt to ever-changing social attitudes and consumer demands. With specific reference to football, Holt (1990: 149) reminds us that 'spectators would frequently adjourn to *football pubs* to discuss the result of the latest match, or the prospect of the next'. Those historical functions still remain in late modern society, and yet it is also important to note that advancements in media technology have coerced pubs to transform once more in order to accommodate the media-driven football revolution of the 1990s. Participant Tim explains:

> Tim: A pivotal part of football has always been going to the pub with my mates before and after the match. Even when I was eighteen and nineteen we were in the away pubs talking to away fans, it was just for the craic and everybody had football in common ... It's only recently really that people watch football in pubs. But like – it's blatantly obvious, if the technology's available then it was always going to be the next logical step for pubs. [Middlesbrough, aged 54 (MF)]

Here, Tim is referring to a media-driven, revolutionary period for football that began in 1992 when the British Sky Broadcasting group (BSkyB[7]) secured the exclusive live rights for televising the newly-created FA Premier League in a

---

7 BSkyB is a public satellite broadcasting company operating in the United Kingdom and Ireland.

deal worth £304 million (Giulianotti 1999). In order to flourish as a business, the plan for BSkyB was dependent on the popularity of top-flight football and subsequently this was used in order to justify the monies paid to the Premier League. Despite initial reservations around a pay-TV system (Sky Sports customers would pay £5.99 per month), it became increasingly evident that consumer demand for the product was strong enough to sustain this business model (Giulianotti, 1999), though in the early days of their production and promotions BSkyB were more effective at targeting businesses, with pubs, bars and clubs making up the bulk of the new custom (Weed 2007). Weed argues that as a consequence of low levels of access to satellite technology in the home, coupled with higher prices charged at live venues and the blanket installation of season ticket methods of payment, many football fans turned to the pub as a form of convenience in order to retain contact with the live performance in an affordable and ad-hoc manner. Brick (2001) makes a similar argument, however, this vision is at odds with participant responses in the current sample:

KD: Why would you say that going to the pub to watch football has gained in popularity?

Graham: People always say that it's all to do with money but I've never thought that. It was more about convincing us that it was worth going ... People forget how hard it was for the landlords ... I mean we all did certain things on a Saturday afternoon. A number of the lads went to the match and some of us did other things that we would do every Saturday or Sunday with the missus or family or whatever it might be. So the landlords had to really try to get you into the pub. So like, if we were drinking on a Tuesday or Friday night or whatever, the landlord at 'The Perry' used to come round and say to us 'You lot coming in for the match tomorrow?' and he'd tempt us with happy hour during the match. [Newcastle, aged 43 (STH)]

The point here is that the gravitation towards watching football in public houses did not simply happen as a consequence of those factors mentioned by Weed or Brick. Participant Graham (above) articulates that going to the pub on a Saturday or Sunday afternoon was anything but convenient to his routine practice at this particular time. Landlords, he suggests, had to work hard to ensure steady custom during these periods using a blend of local marketing and personal persuasion. Hence, there was an initial interdependency between the pub and Sky sports broadcasts, with the success of Sky Sports partially dependent on the public house trade. Furthermore, the commercial success of pubs (through the showcasing of live football) was often dependent on the modernisation of the internal space within the pub. Nowhere was this more apparent than in the propagation of TV screens within public house establishments:

Darren: ... But like, once the facilities got better and pubs tried to change the layout for football, it kind of took off ... I remember in the early days being crowded around one telly in my local. To be honest it was shit, but that's all there was. About a thirty-inch screen, if that – with loads of blokes crowded around. If you go into the same pub now there's like at least a dozen widescreen TVs and two large screens. [Newcastle, aged 45 (MF)]

Likewise, participants such as Stacey (below) describe the refurbishments to the pub as pivotal for the increasing popularity of this consumer pastime. In some instances it seems as though pubs were prepared to undertake a total re-design in order to remove irregular shaped internal walls and booths to maximise space for 'the big screen'. All modifications were designed to enhance the viewing comfort of the football customer:

Stacey: Big screens have made a massive difference. Loads of pubs have knocked down those quaint traditional designs in favour of the open plan bar ... Everyone knows which pubs have the best layout. So, like, if there's a few of you, you know that you can all sit together and basically just have a drink and a laugh. [Sunderland, aged 29 (MF)]

In addition to the creation of more suitable internal surroundings conducive to a positive consumer experience, the allure of international competition (particularly the European Championship competition 'Euro 96' held in England and broadcast on terrestrial television) was quoted (by those who were old enough to attend pubs at this time) as a major turning point in the popularity of watching football in public houses. Consequently, whilst landlords had to work hard to inspire customers to attend at irregular drinking hours, it seemed that international competition, media hype and associated patriotism were enough to evoke a desire for communal televised consumption in public houses. Indeed, participants were able to draw on vivid memories that stem from this period:

Paul: Euro '96 in my local. I didn't just watch the England games but we used to watch potential competition ... The semi final against Germany and the Quarters against Spain had just a terrific atmosphere. I would say that moments like those probably got people coming back into pubs to watch footie. [Middlesbrough, aged 53 (STH)]

Even conceding the fact that the 1996 European Championships were broadcast on British terrestrial television (and therefore TV license payers had the option to watch those matches at home) a culture for watching live football collectively (away from the live venue) was beginning to develop, amidst which special memories were consumed:

> Helen: England v Scotland was brilliant and Gazza's goal and what was it? The dentist's chair.[8] That was brilliant … We stayed in the pub all day after that game. Fantastic game … The good thing about the pub is that you can immediately continue your celebrations, or drown your sorrows and share the experience. [Sunderland, aged 38 (MF)]

In spite of growing enthusiasm for live football consumption in the pub (illustrated above) it should also be noted that some landlords had initially underestimated the commercial potential of hosting live televised football at this time. With reference to the European Championships in 1996, journalist Richard Alan (*The Guardian* 1998[9]) reports that the pub industry had been under-prepared and ultimately overwhelmed by public demand. In the space between Euro '96 and World Cup '98, he reports that pubs underwent some major refurbishments in order to attract football fans into respective establishments. Alan (*The Guardian* 1998) refers to specific elements of theming (in the Disneyisation sense) where for example, 'pubs from the Firkin brewery had spent more than £500,000 on big viewing screens and launched a cast-conditioned beer called Firkin 98, as a reaction to the industry being under-prepared for Euro '96. Furthermore, some pubs such as the Finnesko in Norwich went to extreme lengths 'by turfing the pub and installing stadium seating arrangements'.

In 2002 the World Cup competition was held in Korea and Japan. Taking into consideration the time difference in relation to the UK, this meant that football matches would be shown in the UK between 6am and 12 noon. In spite of this, the desire to consume England's matches within the pub environment remained strong. Explanations for this trend tended to focus on a need for shared communal experience, as Weed (2007: 404) clarifies:

> Voices as disparate as the Lord Chief Justice and the British Beer and Pub Association were highlighting their perception that pubs provide 'atmosphere' for a 'big occasion game as a shared communal experience' and that such occasions are a 'major part of public and pub life' that provide for the collective enjoyment of an event.

---

8 Following a goal against Scotland, Paul Gascoigne celebrated by laying on the floor as if he were sitting in a dentist's chair whilst team mates sprayed water from bottles into his open mouth. This was thought to be in response to an incident before the tournament when England players were photographed on a social night out, drinking alcohol in a dentist's chair.

9 Alan. R. 1998. *The Guardian*, June 7: 66.

'Watching' televised football in a public house or bar was acknowledged for the first time by commercial and professional voices as a consumer activity in its own right. The pub was no longer somewhere that existed purely for football talk (and so-called 'traditional' consumer options) but was now marketed as a space to visually and audibly consume the live performance whilst quenching a thirst for communal experience and adding to narratives of being there:

KD: What makes you want to continue watching football in the pub?

Ruth: I suppose for those big matches, like Boro's Cup Finals over the past ten year, I can tell you exactly where I was and who I was with … So it's saying *I was there* … [Middlesbrough, aged 42 (STH)]

Given that the geographical position of the pub can be situated many miles away from the live performance, the concept of 'being there' for our participants does not necessarily entail a physical journey to the location of the live game. Similarly, Weed (2006) attempts to explain this phenomenon by using Boden and Molotch's (1994) theoretical apparatus 'the compulsion of proximity'. He explains that physical proximity to other likeminded souls (for example, friends and fans of the same team, rather than physical proximity to the live performance) could be equally, if not more important to football fans when searching for desirable and memorable spaces to consume live football. Hence, with a growing plethora of modes through which to consume football, the concept of 'being there' has evolved to mean more than attending the football stadium. Concomitantly, the themed service offered by the public house has evolved in line with the values of corporate television. In turn, this has stimulated a desire for communal viewing that has become synonymous with football culture and routine sociability for many groups of fans. For those, including Bill (below) the communal experience is key to his desire for continued consumption:

Bill: Any Sunderland match that is televised I can't watch at home. I have to go to *the Percy* [pub] to meet the lads … It feels similar to going to the match in some respects, you know, you've got the build-up and the anticipation, the craic with your mates and the enjoyment of the live match. And of course post-match reactions. [Sunderland, aged 34 (MF)]

As a case in point, the compelling desire to consume football at *the Percy* is yet another instance of routine where it was not uncommon to favour one particular venue in which to consume live football. However, in certain instances the desire to consume football in a specific space can extend beyond routine and into ritual, given that fans were shown to associate elements of luck and superstition with specific public houses.

> Jeff: Even though I live about ten miles away I get the bus into Town for Newcastle games. We always go to 'The Volt', it's a lucky pub for us and the atmosphere is great … [Newcastle, aged 27 (MF)]

In a similar vein to the ritualistic chanting that Garry Robson (2000) reports of Millwall fans it seems that ritual was also apparent within the consumption experiences of participants in the current sample. For instance, as well as watching football in lucky pubs (see Jeff, above) rituals can involve a series of events that must be practiced on the day of the match, leading up to the live performance at the pub:

> Wayne: … I used to eat two 'Big Macs' before every game until we stopped winning and I still down a pint [drink a pint of lager in one go] before every game that I watch in the pub. I always think it would make a difference to the result if I never. [Middlesbrough, aged 35 (MF)]

As Wayne (above) suggests, rituals are based on personal superstition with respect to team success and failure ratios. Further, the obsession with attending specific bars for the purpose of watching live televised football illustrates practice that extends beyond the pragmatic. Fans like Jeff (above) can travel miles to his 'lucky' pub in order to consume football in the presence of peers and furthermore, Peter (below) illustrates that, once ingrained, such routines are often maintained where possible, despite inconvenience and economic cost:

> Peter: In about 2005 I moved house to Newcastle for work reasons, so for most televised matches I've got to drive down to my mates and go to the pub in Boro.
>
> KD: Why travel to Middlesbrough?
>
> Peter: Its home isn't it?.. It wouldn't be the same if I watched it by myself in a pub in Newcastle. I always try to watch Middlesbrough games with Middlesbrough supporters. [Middlesbrough, aged 32 (STH)]

Yet again, participant Peter highlights the importance of sociability towards the formation and maintenance of routine bonds. It is worth noting, however, that those bonds are also susceptible to change; and in the current sample this was most frequently evidenced through alterations in personal circumstances and the additional consumer choice that this can bring.

Craig: When I moved house a while back and joined a local team [pub football team] I started watching some Premier League games with my new team mates … I also watch Boro games with a different group of mates somewhere else near Thornaby. So, which ever pub I go to depends on the mates that I go with. [Middlesbrough, aged 27 (STH)]

As well as providing venues for routine and ritual, the pub is also a generic and universal institution, and this is comforting to fans as they negotiate a fandom career. At some stage fans will exercise consumer choice between a variety of public houses that compete with one another for custom. With this it is inevitable that the establishment of new pubs and bars can threaten the custom of existing pubs. They offer new, alluring opportunities to consume in ways that surpass the facilities or conditions currently on offer at any time. The result can be, as in the case of participant Louise (below), a shift in the preferred space to consume live football:

Louise: A new sports bar opened a while back which is better, so we go there now. [Liverpool, aged 20 (MF)]

Notwithstanding this, it was not unusual for fans in the current sample to have two or three possible choices of public house destination that were called upon to suit particular circumstances. From each of the pubs on offer, fans were looking for particular characteristics to optimise the atmosphere for communal viewing with friends, but it is not true that all fans hold universal requirements. Up to this point, and taking into consideration the work of Weed (2006, 2007, 2008), we could be forgiven for thinking that all pubs are loud, boisterous, testosterone-filled spaces reminiscent of old-style terraces. Gibbons and Lusted (2007) provide a typical instance of this when they write about activities within a Cumbrian pub during the 2006 World Cup Finals. They recall:

Rooney was sent off. One man shouted (after punching a wall!) 'Fuck off you Stretford cunt! I'll batter ya!'

This, it must be clear, is not a typical reflection of fandom practice in all public houses across Britain. It is worth pointing out that whilst some participants enjoyed atmospheric pubs, others did not, or on occasion and when the situation dictated, they would sooner find a quiet pub to take in the match, perhaps over a Sunday roast, a singular pint or a pot of coffee:

Richie: I've started taking the wife out for some food to coincide with the match … It's got to the point where I say 'fancy going for some food?' And she'll say 'who are Liverpool playing like?'… It's still good to be out and amongst people if you know what I mean, but I can't take wor lass to some of the other places I go to with the lads from work ... When I go out with her I look for something with, like, a mild atmosphere. [Liverpool, aged 32 (MF)]

Accordingly, the preferred space chosen to consume football is carefully considered and ultimately dependent on the specific social company that participants hold at any given time. Having a meal with a friend, or family member whilst watching the match, is a far different consumer experience from those testosterone-filled spaces described by Weed (2008) and Gibbons and Lusted (2007). This demonstrates once more, the variety and choice of the late modern period and the adaptability of the pub more specifically. For instance, participants, like Paul (below), spoke about his current match-day pub with reference to a choice that he makes between contrasting consumer experiences:

Paul: Just me and my mate Marty go to watch the match in the pub. We've stopped going into town as much and we just stay local ... It's good when the pub has got atmosphere, but we like to be able to hear ourselves talking about the match, so we don't go into any of the daft pubs and we choose a pub with the right atmosphere. [Middlesbrough, aged 53 (STH)]

As in the case above, fans weigh up their options as consumers and chose from the vast array of public houses that can accommodate them. For fans of lower division teams, however, the choice of consumption (that is, the coverage of televised football) in pubs can be a frustrating one.

Wanda: If our televised games coincide with any other games the pubs don't show ours. For example, we were playing on Monday night but Newcastle was on Setanta, so our game wasn't played [televised] anywhere. You could go to six pubs and they'd all be showing the same game which is quite frustrating. [Darlington, aged 21 (STH]

In an attempt to appeal to the mass consumer audience, it seems that public houses (for example, outside of the immediate local area of the affected football club) fail to recognise lower level football and this can be a source of frustration for those directly affected. Participants from lower level teams still enjoyed live televised fixtures between more successful English teams, but they also tended to have a stronger reliance on other modes of media, and newer forms of Sports News channels that offer live consumer information about all teams, irrespective of level:

Luke: The radio is something that I listen to religiously for our away games. But if that's not possible I will watch Sky sports news, even though we hardly get mentioned, at least you can find out if any goals have been scored and how other teams in your league are doing. [Hartlepool, aged 21 (STH)]

Lisa: If you're in the pub, quite a few bars have got the capacity to play Sky Sports News and a Sky sports match on different TVs. See, Sky Sports News is on freeview so pubs can put them both on at the same time and this way everyone knows what's going on around the country. [Darlington, aged 20 (STH)]

In summary, the public house is a site for football consumption that is constantly reinvented to cater for the desires of their consumers. Pubs are fluid and flexible and consequently, as institutions they are relatively stable features of football fandom culture that continue to embrace technology and instigate new consumption routines. Notwithstanding the popularity of televised football and its concomitant relationship with the pub, other forms of new media are also transforming football fandom culture (Boyle and Haynes 2004, Cleland 2009, 2010, Gibbons and Dixon 2010). In what follows I consider the rise of internet technology and its place within the routine consumer experiences of my participants.

Internet Technology and Football Fandom Consumption

Each day fans visit various sports web sites, participate in fantasy sports, celebrate and criticise teams, players, and sporting cultures on blogs, in discussion groups, and on list serves, and gain joyful pleasure in playing sports video games. Each of these media, to varying degrees, embody what has become known as new media, a catch all phrase that includes everything from the internet and e-commerce, to the Blogosphere, video games, virtual reality and other examples in which media technologies are defined by increasing accessibility, fluidity, and interactivity (Leonard 2009: 2).

The situation, as described by Leonard (above), demonstrates some new media consumer experiences that are endured by fans in late modern life, with 'the internet' as the focal point. Historically speaking, Mann and Stewart (2000) have traced the growing use of the internet as it has gained popularity and they have documented that, in the period between 1969 and 1999 the number of computers connected to the internet had risen from four to 56,218,000 and this, they suggest, continues to rise year on year. Accordingly, recent figures from the Office for National Statistics (2007[10]) state that: 'In 2007, nearly fifteen million

---

10 Office for National Statistics. (2007) 'Households with access to the internet, GB'. Available at: http://statistics.gov.uk/cci/nugget.asp?id=8 (accessed November 2007).

households in Great Britain (61 percent) had internet access. This is an increase of just over one million households (seven percent) over the period of one year, and nearly four million households (thrity-six percent) since 2002'. However, so as not to mislead, one must also acknowledge a variety of socio-economical factors that are thought to result in unequal access to new media technologies. For instance, Davis and Duncan (2006) imply that 'class' can influence access to new media, whilst Katz, Rice and Apsden (2001) and others such as Selwyn (2004) report that differences in access still exist across 'age', household 'income' and 'education'. Together those factors contribute towards a digital divide, and yet this notion was not true of participants in the current study (all claiming to have regular access to the internet). Such findings could be coincidental, though it may indicate, as Warde (2004) suggests, that competent practitioners will always attempt to avail themselves with the consumables (that is, services and appropriate tools) relating to any particular practice. Perhaps then, rather than relating in a straightforward sense to issues of economic deprivation, internet access can be one of practice-specific necessity:

KD: Do you have access to the internet?

Charlene: I rely on it! Seriously, how else can I get the information that I need when I need it. It's became my main form of reference. [Newcastle, aged 21 (STH)]

KD: Does it cost you much to access to the internet?

Charlene: No. That's the beauty of it. I'm not exactly well off, but I can afford a computer for the house and I don't even pay a monthly subscription. Coz, I get connected to the internet 'free' as part of my mobile phone package.

As Charlene suggests, the internet has become a reliable source of information-gathering for football fans and this position is supported by the results of a recent European Football survey. The author of this survey, Sandvoss (2005), notes that the predominant use of the internet by sports fans is to gain immediate access to results, match reports, current news and background information. Secondly, he indicates that the internet is used to follow live sporting events via video, audio and textual commentary and finally, the purchasing of merchandise and gambling through online activities forms a third, yet marginal, group of online services. Although Sandvoss has his eye on a more theoretical discussion regarding the coverage of sport and the development of communications technology, he provides valuable information about the everyday use of the internet by football fans as they attempt to gratify an instantaneous thirst for information. Whilst the internet does not cause the thirst for information that Sandvoss describes, it is complimentary to this habitual need:

> Ruth: I've got my favourites[11] set up on all different football sites. Every morning I go through all the sites and get as much information as I can really ... You can't tell me that people up and down the country aren't doing this when the boss isn't looking. [Middlesbrough, aged 42 (STH)]

Ruth sets the scene as she sees it. Personal computers and work stations in offices, libraries, and internet cafes are set with various short-cut commands that have been earmarked by individual fans for the purpose of consuming the world of professional football and creating news that fans themselves begin to disseminate amongst close-knit fandom groups and beyond. Participant Alan (below) contends that as soon as there is any breaking news, he is contacted by peers immediately via email or text message:

> Alan: As soon as there's any news I get it on email straight away and if not on email on text ... If Mike Ashely [Owner of Newcastle United at the time of writing] so much as wipes his arse, I know about it immediately, put it that way. [Newcastle aged 29 (STH)]

Sourcing information of this type has become a routine aspect of daily life for some and a firm part of peer interactions. The internet enables the subtle maintenance of contact between peer groups across occupations as they go about the working week. Participant Craig explains:

> Craig: For me it's a daily ritual. I get into work at about 8:30am and grab a coffee and a bacon sandwich; log into the computer and then check out the sports news ... The news sites. Sky Sports and the BBC are the main ones, or the newspapers ... If there's any worthwhile craic, I'll forward it on by email with a link to the news story ... It usually gets a response from several people and they might say 'yeah, but have you seen so and so' and they'll send a link to whatever they've found ... We continue chatting at intervals all day. [Middlesbrough, aged 27 (STH)]

> KD: What type of newspapers do you look for online?

> Craig: Nationals online, but I have the local delivered most days.

---

11 'Favourites' refers to a shortcut system for personal computers allowing direct access to specifically chosen internet websites.

The active search for practice-specific knowledge is nothing new, and yet with the advancement and encroachment of new media into all aspects of everyday life, the political economy of football has altered the way fans search for this information (Cleland 2010). Internet usage has become a predominant part of popular culture with fans, like Craig (above), choosing to keep abreast of national newspapers online. However, the emergence and popularity of new media does not necessarily result in the disbandment of the older sources, such as local newspapers and radio, though they too have been forced to react to market pressures created by the newer ones (Cleland 2009). For instance, online versions of print newspapers provide the opportunity for agents to browse through items of interest on their computer screen rather than physically buying the latest edition. As Dart (2009: 110) points out, newsprint stories often engender a form of participatory democracy through regular invitations to their viewers to 'tell us what you think', followed by a text or email address so that the readers can send in their comments. Concomitantly those comments become newsworthy, portraying a collective view of any one readership and stamping authority on the perceptions of any given reporter. Moreover, in relation to Craig (above), it is not inconceivable to think that football fans will consume information via both ingrained habitual avenues for consumption and 'new media' methods. In late modern life those modes are increasingly interconnected, and as Cleland (2009: 426) clarifies in a study featuring 827 questionnaires completed by football fans:

> When supporters were asked to name their single most important source for news and information on their club … the local evening newspaper was stated. This therefore, supports the continuation of the historic interdependent relationship between clubs and the local newspaper. However, to highlight the growth of the new media, the official club website was a close second in terms of club news and information.

Cleland (above) draws attention to the continuation of historic modes of consumption for the purpose of information gathering but also acknowledges the emergence of new technologies that are causing modifications to practice. Similarly, the empirical evidence gathered throughout this book serves to substantiate the position that routine acts of consumption are relatively stable in the sense that they are rooted by habitus (that is, they have historical and cultural reference points) and yet, late modern habitus has the potential to be reflexive and open to change.

Football Fandom and Online Sociability

Wanda: Me and my football friends probably keep in touch more online than we do in any other way. And when, say, we go to the pub together we talk about the internet links that we send each other. [Darlington, aged 21 (STH)]

To explain how the internet has become a routine form of consumption for many fans, Dart (2009) draws attention to the importance of new internet software (e.g. such as Wordpress, Blogger, LiveJournal, and Typepad), as a main protagonist that has enabled the creation of blogs. In turn this has allowed for real-time and multiple-way communications between interest groups. These developments have certainly afforded sports fans an opportunity to take a more participatory role in the information exchange process. Subsequently it is possible for fans to become producers of their own stories through social networking sites, as well as consuming what others have written about them in the mainstream media (Dart 2009, Hills 2007). Technologies can therefore increase the accessibility, fluidity and interactivity of the practice and concurrently there are more sites for fans to express themselves and to share views:

KD: Do you like reading or getting involved with some of the fan blogs?

Ian: Yeah, it's good because you get some real 'passionate' debates that mean a lot to whoever is posting ... sometimes some decent points are made and you think 'yeah, they've got a point'. [Darlington, aged 26 (MF)]

'Passion', according to Ian is conspicuous enough, even in the virtual world of blogging, to stimulate feelings of connectivity whilst simultaneously fuelling ammunition for football chat. Unlike the consumer act of watching football in the pub and the prophesised compulsion for physical proximity (described earlier in this chapter), the use of football blogs tends to suggest that proximity to others can also be imagined in the sense that Anderson (1991) would express. Fans can be separated by hundreds if not thousands of miles, and yet this matters not to the football blogger. Rather, it is knowing that others are present (somewhere in the blogosphere) and that they have taken the time to consume and discuss aspects of practice that resonates with participants:

KD: Would you say that online conversations between fans on message boards are affected by the lack of physical presence? Are they less meaningful?

Richie: No, I wouldn't say so, no. You don't have to be in the same room to make it more real ... The topics are real and the responses are more thought out than you get normally. So no, it's not less meaningful and you could argue they are better quality ... You're talking to football fans that are sat in front of a computer, that's the only difference for me but they are all there in the moment chatting to one another and clearly care about the team. [Liverpool, aged 32 (MF)]

Richie (above) illustrates that conversational topics and feelings of emotional intensity are not diluted by the anonymity of the web, and moreover as Matty (below) explains, internet blogs and discussion forums offer a practical solution for some to retain a fix of communication despite geographical proximity.

Matty: ... we all have busy lives but we always make time for football don't we? ... If say, you work long hours, or you live away from your friends like me, then the internet is the perfect resource. It keeps me part of the scene. [Middlesbrough, aged 32 (STH)]

The fact that other fans were poised in front of a computer screen, blackberry or iphone (modes of e-consumption rather than face-to-face interaction) was irrelevant to participants like Matty (above). Internet posts were conceived of as being heavily inflected with identity, cultural capital, commitment, security and a shared experience based on emotional connections to one's team. Thus, the key motives for routine action online were consistent with other offline or physical world consumption routines.

Erasing Myths of Disjunction between Online and Offline Fandom

In the same way that participants have suggested that the internet is an essential consumer source that allows football fans to communicate with one another, it is worth pointing out that academics too are beginning to explore the potential similarities between online and offline conversational discourse. Moving beyond those typologies of fandom that make clear distinction between online and offline worlds (noted in Chapter 3) authors such as Gibbons and Dixon (2010: 606) observe that football blogs retain most of their common offline discourse in an online format. They write:

... boyish banter, narcissistic chanting, singing, and rants of passionate but often disorganised soccer crowds putting forth forceful and passionate opinions (with little emotive regard for feelings of rebutters or opposing fans) are commonplace.

Other studies too draw comparable similarities between online and offline modes of communication including: Johnes' (2007) use of interactions on a discussion forum for Swansea City FC fans (a Welsh team who play in the English Coca-Cola League One) to highlight debates on anti-Englishness and racism amongst fans; Ruddock's (2005) study of fans' online responses to the controversial signing of Lee Bowyer by the English Premier League club West Ham United in 2003; and Millward (2006) and Levermore and Millward's (2007) studies of Liverpool FC fans' interactions regarding the outlines of a European identity emerging through club message board postings and e-zine discussion topics. These authors make the point that online and offline communications are not mutually exclusive, and in the current sample participants held similar perspective.

> Lisa: I joined a Facebook group called the League Two group which is people who support different teams in the league. So if I go to an away game I meet them in the bar. It's actually a really good way to meet people and talk League Two football. [Darlington, aged 20 (STH)]

The above adds partial support to the work of Rheingold (1993: 3) who notes that 'people in virtual communities do just about everything people do in real life, but leave their bodies behind'. This statement is convincing in the sense that virtual communities are versatile and comparable to everyday life and yet participants were able to take this notion a step further. In the example above, the concepts 'virtual' and 'real life' are almost indistinguishable from one another, given that physical bodies and virtual entities have become part of the same series of consumption activities. Kirsty explains:

> Kirsty: We got chatting on the Facebook group and met up a few times socially. Four of us now share a car to go to the games. We live quite close but had never really met before … It saves us all some money. [Hartlepool, aged 33 (STH)]

Since both Kirsty and Lisa (above) are season ticket holders at their respective clubs, further support can be offered to substantiate those claims suggesting that fans who participate in (and thus consume) so-called 'traditional' and 'authentic' fandom practices (for example, match-day attendees) are often the same fans who contribute to online discussion forums, blogs, email loops and message boards. Accordingly, evidence points in the direction of Crawford (2004) and Bell (2007), both of whom criticise the presence of an online/offline dichotomy in relation to fandom, suggesting instead that social, economic and cultural interactions occur simultaneously in cyberspace and make up part of what we call 'everyday life'.

Perhaps the most explicit example to provide empirical support for this argument comes from Palmer and Thompson's (2007) ethnographic study of a group of Australian Rules Football fans named 'the Grog Squad'. Through field research the authors reveal the mutual importance of internet communications and real life interactions for this specific fan base. They explain that for the Groggies, the internet provided a crucial mechanism through which fans maintained their particular cultural identity (with a larger proportion of communication occurring this way) and moreover, it was also noted as a site for organisation of 'real time' meetings that would occur later. Consequently, the authors add support to the contention that the hypothesised and stereotypical portrayal of internet users as inauthentic fans (that is, chat room nerds or geeks that are lacking the capacity for meaningful social interaction in the real world) is false. Rather, they insist 'the fact that the Groggies also have ongoing, real time contact sits in opposition to other studies of fans for which the internet is their principle form of communication' (Palmer and Thompson 2007: 197).

In addition to fans that interact comfortably online (like the Groggies), the current sample is also inclusive of those who prefer to read online posts but choose not to interact. The regularity of access to blogs, discussion forms, fanzines and e-zines remained strong for those participants, but they would consume information without posting any comments or interacting with other bloggers at all. I have labelled such participants 'online voyeurs' given that they were able to carve out an intimate yet distanced voyeuristic consumer position without interactive involvement in the virtual realm. Take the following comments from participants Dave and Colin as examples:

Dave: I have a look at forums but I don't get involved, I just like to read what other people write … It's funny I love reading it. [Newcastle, aged 40 (STH)]

Colin: Teesside Tommy is like one of these blogs and people send all these blogs in about football and Teesside Tommy sort of replies to them. It's alright. It's just fans' views on whatever's happening at the time, transfers and all that. It's a good laugh to read, but I don't write in or anything. [Middlesbrough, aged 53 (STH)]

Deriving a sense of satisfaction from regularly viewing what is pleasing to them, online voyeurs are hungry to consume information but lack the inclination to get personally involved in online conversations. Hence the routine (for those described here) involves consuming the lives and experiences of others and this, in turn, offers the sentiment of socialising without actual engagement. In addition to this and in relation to the concept of ontological security, it appears that online voyeurism can provide a safety net for maintenance of contact with likeminded fans that one perceives to share a common bond:

Nats: The only reason I enrol on some websites is to become an online stalker … it's cool because you find out what's going on and what people are saying about the Boro. [Middlesbrough, aged 24 (STH)]

121

Despite the balance of active or inactive consumption that fans may take part in when consuming football via the internet, the single most goal of participants was to further acquisition of knowledge. Of course, some participants were clearly more advanced than others in their use and navigation of this new media resource. A general trend to emerge suggests age differentiation in terms of internet use where younger participants, it seems, had embraced and integrated new media into the practice to a greater extent than older participants who tended to make tentative use of the internet, often for its simplistic functions. Older participants were self admittedly more resistive of the internet and therefore the familiarity and use of this resource was less well-established. Those findings are congruent with the suggestion of Wellman and Gulia (1998: 170) that online interaction is informed by the baggage that individuals bring to the computer 'including stage of life' and 'offline connections with others'. This is something that clearly resonates with Jimmy, a participant with limited technological skills:

> Jimmy: I have only really just started to use it but have found it to be really useful. My son got it in for me [installed it at home] and showed me the best sites for football. I use it every day but it still takes me a while to click on the right things … I'm getting there but I'm not as fast as the young ones … It's definitely a part of fandom but it's not a part that I could have imagined thirty years ago. [Newcastle, aged 55 (MF)]

Jimmy illustrates the point that offline connections with computer-literate relations or friends, are important for the transferability of knowledge and the embracement of new technology-laden modes of consumption. This in turn has implications for theoretical discussions in relation to practice. For instance, it true that knowledgability can be passed from one generation to the next in an active and reciprocal way (discussed in Chapter 5) but the transfer of knowledge is not always uni-directional. As in the example above new forms of consumption (that is, those which are technologically-driven) are, generally speaking, embraced to a greater extent by younger generations that are still forming their routines within the practice. It follows then, that younger members of any practice have a role to play by inevitably teaching older members how to cope with and embrace change:

> Stacey: My dad was useless with technology and a real sceptic but I've looked after him. I've shown him the basics and he's at a point when he's comfortable plodding along. But like anything that pops up, he's straight on the phone saying 'Stace what does this mean'? or whatever. You know, he panics at times [laughing] … He does ok really – but that's down to my patience. [Sunderland, aged 29 (MF)].

Of course, technological change has the potential to disrupt feelings of practice security for agents like Stacey's father, yet gentle introductions to new technologies derived through interactions with others often help to soften the blow. Concomitantly, new routines are formed on the back of new knowledge and so the practice gradually evolves.

Chapter Summary

Through the words of participants, this chapter has uncovered some of the routine elements of football fandom consumption and consequently, it has inferred the importance of routine to both the maintenance and evolution of fandom culture. With reference to the maintenance of routine practice, a number of underlying motives were discussed as derivatives of one's habitus. For instance, routine acts of consumption were used by participants to maintain social relationships, to act as markers of masculinity, to increase knowledgability and to reaffirm authenticity.

However, in contrast to those seemingly solid features of fandom habitus, participants did unwittingly point to transformations in routine and the potential fluidity that exists for fans as they make consumption choices across time and space. Changes in technology were noted and often embraced by participants, merging seamlessly into descriptions of daily routines. Subsequently new actions become 'authentic' markers of fandom practice and modes of capital accumulation. Accordingly, in conjunction with Giddens (1984), the evidence presented in this chapter demonstrates how routine or seemingly trivial daily acts of consumption (given that they are practiced most frequently) have a profound influence on the generality of social action within the lives of late modern football fans.

Chapter 7
Conclusion

At this point it is useful to recapitulate some of the basic ideas contained in the preceding chapters in order to highlight the main tenets of my argument. First and in contrast with much of the existing literature, it is important to clarify that this book has not aimed to capture the exceptional elements of football fandom (for example, hooliganism, obsession, racism) that are well documented elsewhere. Rather, it has presented a sociology of mundane consumption experiences that make up football fandom cultures and paradoxically this is what is exceptional about it. More specifically I have argued that football fandom equates to a fluid series of routine consumption activities that are practiced in the course of everyday life. The line of argument taken is that those routine, trivial or seemingly mundane consumption activities have a pronounced influence on the construction, maintenance and evolution of football fandom cultures. Furthermore, it contends that football fandom is an organic phenomenon that is slowly moving boundaries of authenticity based on the reflexivity of practicing agents as they participate in and respond to the demands of consumer life.

Conscious not to disconnect football fandom culture from wider social developments across time and space, in Chapter 2 I began by arguing that spectator football has always involved forms consumption. Accordingly, when authors have implied that capitalist exploitation of football fandom is a new phenomenon that stands in contrast to the idea of 'traditionality', I suggest that this has only served to create a false premise on which to base theoretical ideas. Consequently in Chapter 3 I have argued that there is a need for a more sophisticated analysis of football fandom that seeks to understand how individual action is organised within mundane, everyday consumption activities whilst simultaneously recognising structural features that are reproduced through individual practice. Chapters 4–7 were used to advance this argument via an examination of evidence from the world of contemporary football fandom. Proceedings were set in motion with research into the genesis of football fandom cultures.

The Genesis of Football Fandom Cultures and the Consumption of Knowledge

With reference to the genesis of football fandom and the consumption of knowledge, findings (outlined in Chapter 4) indicate that parents and peers were the most dominant influences for participants. First and most predominantly, fandom was described by many as an inherited, transmissible practice and a slow process of autonomization involving the consumption of knowledge, discourse and social norms that were noted to underpin ones perception of the practice. Thus, following Bourdieu (1984, 1990) it seems that football fandom cultures are, for the most part, self-perpetuating in the sense that communities of taste stem from self propagating histories of consumption activities based on objective social conditions and accrued personal experiences. Briefly revisiting previous statements from participants can help to substantiate those contentions made here.

Take for instance Luke's discussion of fandom as a 'rite of passage' (p. 49); Bill's declaration that football is a 'form of normality' for males (p. 39); or Lisa's assertion that football fandom is a 'consequence of heredity' (p. 49). Within those incidences the power of self-propagation is revealed and when combined with discussions of parenting, a process of conscious coercion was noted by some participants towards their children's involvement in the practice. Consistent with Bourdieu (1984) these findings illustrate that one's inclination to practice is likely to reflect social circumstance. More specifically, the values, dispositions and practices of significant others are subsumed or modelled, leading to the relative reproduction of previous generation habitus. Equally, in line with Giddens' (1984) concept of practical consciousness, it was clear that participants draw on learnt knowledge to make sense of their current involvement in the practice. One of the most reflexive instances of this was acknowledged by participant Tim and it is worth citing at length:

> Tim: Just like I've done for our Richard [son] he will probably impart his knowledge to his son or daughter in the same way. My Dad certainly taught me everything about football and my love for the Boro came from that. So I can take the credit for getting Richard involved but my father could claim credit for both of us and his dad could take credit after that. You see what I'm saying? You learn it from your dad but it feels natural because by the time you're old enough to think for yourself you're hooked and it's embedded within you. [Middlesbrough, aged 54 years (MF)]

This situation (above) was also true for others, however, it is important to stress that the hereditary experience that Tim (above) explains is not a necessary and sufficient condition that is required in order to consume football as a fan. Consequently, I suggest that caution must be taken not to overemphasise the power of structure or the unopposed continuation of tradition in this respect. I have made it clear in Chapter 5 that habitus (for participants in relation to football fandom) is not the all-encompassing force that Bourdieu would conceive it to be. Despite those elements of predictability (via the coercion of parents and peers) it is evident that late modern society offers no guarantees that coercion will gain the desired effect or that tradition will roll over in such a predictable manner. Take Newcastle United fans Dave and Andy (pp. 51-2) as examples. Both indicate that despite their best efforts to inspire their children to take up the practice, they were unsuccessful in this regard. In fact, this trend was known to reach beyond the current sample given that participants knew of at least one friend or acquaintance whose children did not embrace football culture in the manner that was predicted for them:

> Jeff: My best friend 'Jamesy' is the biggest Sunderland supporter that you've ever met but his kids don't follow football at all ... He took them to the games and stuff but they never did take to it. Strange how it works isn't it? I'd of thought out of all of us, Jamesy's kids would be fanatical. [Newcastle, aged 27 (MF)]

As well as 'opting out' of fandom practice, agents from backgrounds unrelated to football were also shown to have 'opted in' by embracing football culture through vast and various influences that extend beyond one's structural background or habitus. Take for example the potential influence of one's spouse to fuel a partner's interest (as in Carol's situation (p. 53), or the influence of a new acquaintance to change a previously impartial and disinterested agent into a partisan football fan (as Wanda explains, p. 53). Likewise new media technologies (that is, new modes of consumption) were also shown to initiate or awaken the desire for football fandom in persons that have previously displayed little interest. The case where participant Ian (p. 54) describes how a virtual introduction to football via the cult computer game Championship Manager can lead to real life fandom demonstrates that the acquisition of knowledge need not derive itself from objective social conditions. Cultural mediators can broaden ones spectrum for practice by extending the potential of cultural knowledge to an audience beyond 'traditional' communities of taste.

Crucially then, on the evidence presented I argue that the popularised idea of 'traditional communities of taste' (that are thought to be based on class groupings) had limited relevance for fans when making consumer choices. In line with Hennion (2007) taste was described in pragmatic form, often dependent on diverse friendship networks rather than perceived 'traditional' class based groupings. For instance participants Andy (p. 45) and Kate (p. 44) explain how as a result of a varied range of friends from different social backgrounds, they are able to participate comfortably in a wide range of consumer activities. Furthermore, when asked: 'is class an issue that you ever think about when you take part in those diverse activities?'Andy responded:

> Andy: I don't really see it. I don't think it's about class. It's just about interests and knowing how to go on ... I mix in all types of circles and have friends of

all different classes and like I say, everyone just mixes together no problems at all. [Newcastle, aged 50 (MF)]

As reflexive consumers, participants had the ability to change behaviour in accordance with the demands of multiple consumer practices and associated peer groups. The sports football and horse racing entail different social etiquette, and yet Andy describes his capabilities of adapting to the conventions of each without any degree of discomfort. Thus, as Giddens (1991) suggests, lifestyles are in one sense habitual given that they often lead from objective structures; and yet when confronted with new knowledge or when agents come into contact with peers from diverse cultural backgrounds; they have the capacity to reflect on and change behaviour. In this manner, participants have displayed characteristics of what Peterson (1997) has coined 'omnivore' type behaviour in the sense that they have wide-ranging tastes that, in theoretical terms, replace the old assumption of class differentiation. Perhaps then as Peterson argues, the cultural omnivore is becoming more prevalent and is more suited to a consumer based world with less distinct boundaries and greater tolerance of diversity. Paradoxically, however, tolerance of others did not feature in explanations of perceived authenticity.

Findings indicate that fan cultures are sites of internal contestation given that participants understood what they considered authentic practice to be, and this was based on perceptions of 'otherness' gathered from an assortment of eclectic consumption experiences. Thus, fandom was marked by a series of fluid and varied authenticity claims with otherness taking a variety of forms, often contributing to one's descriptions of 'dirt' or 'vulgarity' on behalf of fellow supporters that were perceived to be different. An assortment of judgements were made by the participants and different outcomes were reached, however, it was clear that, in all instances, consumption practices were used momentarily to define those boundaries of otherness.

Fake fandom was one form of characterisation pursued by most interviewees, with lack of loyalty (explained with reference to consumption) constant and definitively present in the construction of 'fake'. Examples of internal contestation of this type were noted through Sarah's account of 'the boo boys', a group that pay to consume live football (that is, offering financial support) but are perceived to be paradoxically and overtly critical of the team (p. 58); Nat's description (p. 58) of 'fickle fans', who are inconsistent in their consumption patterns in the sense that they desert the team after a run of poor results and Linda's account of fans like her boss (p. 58) who have only recently begun to attend games on a corporate ticket but now perceive themselves as 'genuine' against the criteria that Linda subscribes to. Yet, despite the presence of fluid and varied notions of authenticity, it is worth noting that all interviewed fans (regardless of primary mode of consumption or routine consumption experiences) thought themselves to be 'authentic' or 'genuine' with an ability to distinguish between 'real' and 'fake' via the panoptic surveillance of consumption activities. All interviewees felt that they were under the panoptic surveillance of others and likewise, they too stood in judgement of their fellow fans. Take for example Kelly's concern that she is treated differently to male supporters (p. 63); Carl's assertion (p. 60) that only those fans sharing similarities to him are worthy of admiration; or Ruth's contention (p. 60) that there are only certain types of fans that she can identify with based on reflections of consumption and subsequent conceptions of authenticity. Such instances highlight the common effects of self surveillance as it exists for both the replication and reconstitution of one's perceptions of authenticity. Moreover, the use of the panoptic gaze (Foucault 1979) to monitor authenticity invariably contributes to disharmony between same-group fans. For instance, the internalised standards of perceived authenticity or rules of panoptic governance are, in the end, so diverse between varied supporter networks that there are no generic or coherent rules from which to judge authentic behaviour with universal agreement. Given that fans do not share homogenous experiences or ideas of genuineness in relation to perceptions of football fandom practice, it seems appropriate to suggest that authenticity must therefore rest firmly in the eye of the consumer – and on occasion participants were openly reflexive about this issue:

> Tim: Surely there's not much agreement about what a fan is because my perception will be different to say someone who travels to matches home and away, or someone who say supports Manchester United but lives in London. [Middlesbrough, aged 54 (MF)]

Furthermore, because the concept of authenticity invokes feelings of difference and associated anxieties, it is important to note that any deviations from perceived norms (for our participants) were often met and attacked with narratives of otherness. Consequently, they were typified with reference to dirt in the context that social anthropologist Mary Douglas (1966: 40) describes. Social agents, she explains, 'often try to examine or make sense of the behaviour of others in relation to one's own experiences' (for example, causing a degree of dissonance) and thus, difference is often transcribed negatively. This is apparent in Nicola's description of 'glory supporters' (p. 59) to portray those fans who support teams other than that of their home town and Jacko's depiction of 'the Cartoon Army' (p. 64), a group of fans associated with wider negative social stereotypes 'the chavs'. In direct support of Douglas (1966), Jacko explains the inferior nature of chav fans when compared with, what he calls, 'my type of fan':

> Jacko: … Then you've got another set of fans that I would class myself in that mould. Probably more mature than the 'cartoon army', probably higher intelligence and probably a little more sensible with regards to the club taking the piss out of them. My set of fans will ask questions about the conduct of club business

but the cartoon army just bend over and take whatever the club throws at them. [Newcastle, aged 28 (MF)]

Thus, I have explained in Chapter 4 that perceptions of fandom are specifically related to the reality of one's reflexive habitus and hence, they are often reminiscent of unwritten moralistic codes that are specific to this. Consequently, because fans consume the game in specific ways, any deviation from learned norms inevitably questions the practice as they see it. In turn this can cause a degree of anxiety which can be momentarily or temporarily soothed by adapting or praising specific depictions of authenticity (the moral 'we') over otherness (the immoral 'them'). In addition and yet in a contradictory fashion, fans were able to think past internal variations in order to highlight perceptions of coherence or togetherness when the situation dictates. Conceptions of 'us' and 'them' can change rapidly within the imagination of the football fan in response to outside threats and romanticised visions of imagined communities. For instance Colin (p. 68) makes reference to 'shared values' and Nats (p. 67) to the 'community' of like-minded supporters, which, when taken together with those clear divisions between perceptions of authenticity leads to a situation where fragmentation and togetherness were often noted by participants as two sides of the same coin. For example, participant Colin reiterates:

> Colin: I know I've slaughtered some fans of this club but in the end I am a proud fan and they're proud fans … One thing Boro fans have got in abundance is pride in our team and pride in our town! [Middlesbrough, aged 53 (STH)]

So, despite differentiation, perceptions of otherness and sameness were mutually and for the most part, nonsensically intertwined, conjuring opposite responses of aversion and affection to one another respectively. In other words, football fans were not always consistent with perceptions of authenticity (based on type and extent of consumption activities) but all shared the idea that the majority of fans were 'like them'. Hence, the imagined community of like-minded fans was acknowledged despite obvious differences between accounts and experiences on scholarly inspection.

Disneyisation and Football Fandom Culture

Using Bryman's (2004) concept of Disneyisation, in Chapter 5 I have explained that football fandom cultures are affected by changes in marketing, advertising and the delivery of commercial goods and services. Thus, beyond the consumption of knowledge and the panoptic surveillance of others, it is argued that football fandom cultures are also influenced by external corporate pressures that seep into and integrate seamlessly with everyday fandom practice. Accordingly, I have argued that football fandom practice has gradually evolved to contain a variety of 'themed experiences' that are heavily inflected with the external dynamics of the market. Furthermore, it is apparent that those experiences have become naturalised and accepted by many participants as part of 'normal' cultural practice, though some do not consider change as desirable. For instance, participant Jimmy (aged 55) explains: 'It's not fandom like I remember it … I liked it the way it was before it was sold to the punters like a fairground'. The fairground that Jimmy refers to demonstrates the way that commercial theming has altered the practice (for this participant) and moreover, he explains how this contradicts his original perception of authenticity. Conversely, others, like Suzi favourably refer to elements of Disneyisation such as themed executive packages that are available for affluent football fans; Rhona and Andy (pp. 79-80) too, discuss the merits of hybrid consumption opportunities within the stadium; and Jacko, Ben and Nicola illustrate the growing commercial enterprise occurring in the geographical area surrounding the club grounds.

> Nicola: On the doorstep to St. James' Park there is Eldon Square for all of your shopping, and we now have 'The Gate' that caters for all types of fans.[1] There's restaurants, and a Wetherspoons that do drink as well. It's a good family friendly atmosphere away from the men's pre-match entertainment, 'the strippers' in the Bigg Market. It's also got a multiplex cinema and on match days they run a cycle of films that finish in time for kick off.

So, whether favourable or not, participants were clear that business ideology has infiltrated and consequently altered the match-day experience by virtue of creating a variety of consumer options that have become accepted by many fans as part of 'normal' practice. Evidence suggests therefore, that perceived 'authentic' experiences of football fandom are becoming more dependent on the consumption of wider consumer experiences, which infiltrate, invade and eventually embody perceptions of match-day authenticity. Consequently, with many additional options besides, the football ground has become a crucible of choice and consumption that participants both expect and for the most part, desire:

> Helen: Football grounds are much better than they used to be. We are spoilt really. The facilities are so nice and well maintained … it's just a nice place to watch the match with all your creature comforts.

---

1 The Gate (opened in 2002) has nineteen venues spread across three floors, including a twelve screen Empire Cinema and Aspers Casino. The Gate is also next to Newcastle's Chinatown, famous for oriental restaurants.

KD: The facilities are up to standard then?

Helen: Fantastic facilities. But that's what's expected now. There's loads to keep us occupied … It's designed to keep the customers happy. [Sunderland, aged 38 (STH)]

Consumption is sustained, it seems, through the perceived emotional congruence that exists between the fan, market products and the club. In accordance with Giddens (1984), this relationship is played out and reconstituted by agents as they unwittingly contribute to 'unintended consequences' of social interactions. In this instance, the unintended consequences to which I refer relate specifically to the self-entrapment of football fans as regular and routinised consumers (Illous 2009). This was most notable where participants did not understand themselves to have simple market choices. As Alan[2] suggests 'we're treated worse than consumers because … people know we're not going to support Man United … they know we'll never support anyone else'. Thus, even when dissatisfied with the club or performances of the team, it was apparent that fans still felt an overriding, compelling desire to consume based on an inelastic emotional commitment to the team. As participant Stephen suggests *'it's like we can't help ourselves'*.[3]

On this evidence, it becomes apparent that as well as being pragmatic (Chapter 4) taste is also derived from ongoing, intense feelings or emotions acquired and acted out through processes of consumption. This was expressed through those emotional connections that were attributed to otherwise inanimate material commodities:

KD: Why do you buy the shirt every season?

Stuart: Well I love the club obviously and the shirt is the club … It's just the passion I have for West Ham. That's what the shirt is. It shows who I am and what's important … It's not just the shirt … the 1975 FA Cup original programme is priceless to me. It's something I show people when they come around … If there was a fire, I'd be more bothered about saving that to be honest.

KD: Really?

Stuart: Well I've had it and looked after it for years. It's part of my history and my club's history.

---

2 Alan [Newcastle, 29 (STH)].
3 Stephen [Sunderland, 27 (MF)].

The purchasing of an item of this type is only the beginning of a utilitarian or emotional relationship with the commodified product. Only on appropriation do material goods (emblazoned with the club badge) become infused with meaning beyond their economic or use value. Take participant Lee (p. 92) and his collection of official and unofficial paraphernalia (that is, programmes, beer mats and bus tickets) that were gathered on a trip to watch Middlesbrough FC in the 2006 UEFA Cup final. Those items were paid for and then, on appropriation, they were re-designed into a collage, framed and wall-mounted in the home to document the adventure of watching his club. Such examples are illustrations of what Willis (1990) has coined 'grounded aesthetics' in the sense that affective and innovative attachments are made and reconstituted in line with the capitalist market and the ever increasing plethora of new commodities. As Willis explains, capitalist culture has unwittingly provided tools for further symbolic expression given that commodities have rapidly became a symbolic aspect of everyday life. Thus, when appropriated in creative ways, commodities are loosened from their origins. This process then accentuates emotional connections to those commodities and further intensifies the cyclical relationship between emotion and sustained material consumption throughout one's football fandom career.

The Significance of Routine Football Consumption

Routine consumption behaviours were an inevitable feature of everyday life for the participants within this sample and they had profound implications towards feelings of ontological security. Whether attending the match, buying a newspaper, watching specific television programmes, stopping for a drink at the pub or predicting the first goal scorer, participants have shown how routine procedures can protect agents from feelings of anxiety and conversely, they were able to demonstrate how anxieties are caused when routines are broken. For example, participant Martin refers to the first time that he broke with routine (for example, not attending a live home fixture in order to take his girlfriend shopping). He recalls: 'the overriding emotion was … I felt lost, I just felt anxious'.

Whilst feelings of security can be breached in this way, all participants attempted to minimise feelings of anxiety (subsidising activities such as watching the match) through the routine consumption and dissemination of relevant football related information, expressed as a crucial part of everyday discursive practice. Researching and keeping up to date with football-related gossip or 'football chat' was explained by all as a fundamental part of being a fan. Whether as a form of light-hearted dark humour amongst friends (see Rachael p. 103) or workmates (see Colin, p. 104), or even as a polite introductory topic of conversation between unfamiliar acquaintances (see Keith, p. 101), routine football chat was shown to feed feelings of security by establishing and reaffirming relationships; acting as markers of masculinity; increasing knowledgability and reinforcing emotional connections. Yet, for all of this stabilising quality, it was noted that the recursive nature of routine behaviours does not always result in an endless repetition of practice within football cultures. As discussed in Chapter 5, external factors including new modes of consumer choice and technological advancements can change the dynamics of football fandom cultures by creating new innovative opportunities for fans to consume with regularity. To illustrate this point, in Chapter 6 I have drawn attention to the growing popularity of watching live televised football in public house venues and the adoption of 'the internet' as new forms of fandom practice – thus acknowledging the emergence of new form of routine or 'tradition' where none had previously existed.

In relation to the latter mode, the internet was specifically noted by participants as an important foundation for frequently sourced information or even as a primary source for social interactions between fans. This supports the work of Leonard (2009) and Cleland (2010), both of whom recognise the increasing accessibility, fluidity and interactive qualities of the internet with its capacity to move fans towards participatory democracy in areas that were previously associated with passive fandom. Furthermore, I have explained how, in many instances, virtual and physical life become almost indistinguishable from one another as physical bodies and virtual entities can become part of the same practice. For example, meeting others online via mainstream social network sites (such as Facebook) and transferring relationships into the physical world as demonstrated by participants Lisa (p. 120) and Kirsty (p. 120) illustrate how 'real life' and 'virtual interactions' can become intertwined in practice. Such examples help to build evidence against those theoretical propositions that speak of an online/offline split where offline communications are regarded as authentic and online communications inconsequential. I have argued instead, that the internet provides an extension of the everyday consumer experience of football fandom. Subsequently, it is apparent that those fans participating in what scholars have previously considered as 'traditional activities' (for example, such as attending a live match) are often the same fans that contribute to online discussion forums, blogs, email loops and message boards. Of course it should be acknowledged that fans do not always embrace the internet in the same way. Whilst some use this resource for multiple way communications, others seek out information without interacting, and even the older members of this sample (that were admittedly sceptical of new technology) were able to act as, and have concomitantly taken comfort from becoming online voyeurs:

> Jimmy: Now I've got it in [that is, the internet has been installed] and I'm getting used to it, it's great. I get all the information from the match and that. Can watch interviews with the managers, you know? All that stuff.

KD: You said you don't chat with other fans though?

Jimmy: Well come on man! A bloke of my age. What's the point of it? I get a good laugh from reading some of it, but I'd rather speak with people face to face.

KD: But you do read what other fans are saying?

Jimmy: Yes, but it's just for my entertainment. [Newcastle, aged 55 (MF)]

The overriding point here is that, as new technology (that is, new modes of consumption) has evolved, it has been subsumed by those agents directly involved in football culture. Once firmly embedded and with the fear factor reduced, participants such as Jimmy (above) have found a new source of information, a new point of contact and consequently a new form of security within the practice that he continues to enjoy. In terms of the transferral of cultural specific information, a further point should be noted here. Whilst it is true that knowledgability can be (and often is) passed from one generation to the next, the transferability of knowledge is not always uni-directional. Hence, new technologies are often embraced by younger generations that are still forming their consumption routines. Consequently, younger members of any practice have their role to play by inevitably teaching older members how to cope with and embrace change. As Stacey (p. 122) explains, her father panics when using new technologies and he relies on her knowledge to rectify any technological hitches and more generally to install his confidence in a new mode of consumption.

Conclusion: Rethinking Football Fandom as Consumption in Late Modern Life

When taken together the preceding chapters of this book have encouraged readers to formulate a picture of football fandom as consumption in the late modern period. Taken from the point of fandom genesis and extending into the most routine and mundane aspects of daily lives, this book has captured the essence of football fandom cultures, both in the moment and as they shift and change with time. It has explored how fandom is consumed through the mechanics of social life and has given space to those micro and macro based influences that help to maintain and evolve this consumer based phenomenon. In doing so this book has acknowledged what acts of consumption 'mean' to fans beyond the simple economic purchase, and this has helped to explain how fans can find themselves embroiled in an emotive culture that is reliant on specific and often implicit understandings of consumption activities relating to themselves and others.

I have argued that to understand the construction, maintenance and evolution of football fandom cultures, an appreciation of the everyday consumption experience is crucial. After all, evidence suggests that the continuity of football cultures is sustained through acts of consumption that are implicit in semi-conscious processes of cultural teachings, supplemented with exchange rituals that run 'down' (for example, from senior agents), 'across' (for example, via peers) and 'up' (for example, from younger agents that adopt new routines) through generations of fans. Consequently the conditions of late modern life were reflected in participant narratives through a desire to, in one sense 'replicate' perceived tradition, whilst simultaneously seeking to 'advance' an updated practice reflective of the late modern period and associated consumer expectations. So whilst it is clear that fandom is practiced and consequently sustained through routine acts of consumption, I would like to highlight the significance of these findings towards the future theorisation of football fandom cultures.

Throughout this book I have argued that there is a need to rethink football fandom for the conditions of late modern life. Rather than theorising at either end of a structure/agency dichotomy as others have, I have argued that football fandom, in all of its component parts, equates to acts of consumption that cannot be explained by structural conditions or individual choice alone. At the crux of my argument I have suggested that contemporary theorists have oversimplified the concept of fandom by basing thoughts, theories, dichotomies and typologies on abstract, popularised conceptual creations rather than on empirical evidence from agents that are directly involved in the field. Concomitantly, I propose that the popularised obsession with 'traditional' and 'new' types of fandom that is still prevalent within much of the literature has negatively obstructed, or gently coerced, authors to derive conclusions from false realities. Hence, I have argued that in the late modern period, we are not witnessing the birth of new types of fandom, or the death of traditional support. Instead we are witnessing something altogether more organic: a social practice in the process of evolution; a way of life that is slowly but surely moving its boundaries towards ever changing ideas of authenticity (based on continued group and individual communications) enacted through consumption. So, rather than using the concepts of 'structure' and 'agency' to theoretically oppose one another by creating a dualistic framework for fandom, this book has demonstrated (through the lived experience of participants) that it is the interplay between those diverse, yet integrative paradigms that provides the key to understanding football fandom cultures in late modern life. For it is the co-existence of perpetuating structural routines (habitual thought processes that result in the maintenance of perceived tradition) and simultaneously one's capacity for reflexivity that best explain the experiences of fans in this sample. Both concepts (structure and agency) were discussed interchangeably through individual narratives of fandom, and thus, in line with Giddens (1984) and Bourdieu (1984), participants described the presence of a 'duality', where structure is not external to individuals but it is chronically implicated in the everyday lives of fans as they interact with one another through modes of consumption. Those modes of consumption can take many forms. They can be materialistic or experiential, intensive or shallow, tacit or discursive, informal or formalised, weakly or strongly sanctioned and yet; when taken together, they contribute to the maintenance and evolution of football cultures by exalting rules to follow and providing conditions for acceptable modes of change. Hence, structures exist within the knowledgeable activities of football fans, which will, over time, be reproduced or altered as properties of football cultures. Consequently, football fandom cultures are both stable and changeable with the enduring success of spectator football attributed to its ability to uphold the notion of tradition whilst slowly adapting to ever-changing social attitudes and consumer demands through the duality of structure.

In summary, this book offers an analysis of football fandom practice that sits between current theories. Rather than theorising at extreme ends of a structure/agency dichotomy or compartmentalising the fandom experience for ease of explanation, it navigates between and merges theoretical perspectives in order to demonstrate that football fandom practice cannot be explained by structural conditions or individual choice alone. Moreover, whilst previous research into football fandom (that is, using Horne's 2006: 36 summary) would tend to position fans as either 'communicators' (Giulianotti 2002); 'victims' (Sandvoss 2003), 'dupes' (King 1998, 2002), or 'rational actors' (Crawford 2004) – I argue that they can be all of the above, sometimes simultaneously, as agents negotiate and contend with multifaceted daily lives. In other words, football fandom cultures are fluid and ever-changing in line with those everyday experiences of football fans. They are 'constructed' via consumption experiences and 'maintained' and 'altered' because of them.

Bibliography

Adams, M. 2006. Hybridizing habitus and reflexivity: Towards an understanding of contemporary identity? *Sociology*, 40(3), 511-28.

Adkins, L. 2002. *Revisions: Gender and Sexuality in Late Modernity*. Buckingham: Open University Press.

Alasuutari, P. 1995. *Researching Culture: Qualitative Method and Cultural Studies*. London: Sage.

Appleton, A. 1961. *Hotbed of Soccer: The Story of Football in the North-East*. London: Rupert Hart-Davis.

Anderson, B. 1991. *Imagined Communities: Reflections on the Origins and Spread of Nationalism*. London: Verso.

Armstrong, G. 1998. *Football Hooligans: Knowing the Score*. Oxford: Berg.

Armstrong, G. and Harris, R. 1991. Football hooliganism: Theory and evidence. *Sociological Review*, 39(2-3), 427-58.

Arnold, A. 1989. The belated entry of professional soccer into the West Riding Textile District of Northern England: Commercial imperatives and problems. *The International Journal of the History of Sport*, 6(3), 319-34.

Back, L., Crabbe, T., and Solomos, J. 2001. *The Changing Face of Football: Racism, Multiculturalism and Identity in the English Game*. Oxford: Berg.

Bale, J. 1978. Geographical Diffusion and the Adoption of Professionalism in Football in England and Wales. *Geography*, 63(3), 188-97.

Bale, J. 1993. *Sport, Space and the City*. London: Routledge.

Banyard, P. and Shevlin, M. 2001. Responses of football fans to relegation of their team from the English Premier League: PTS? *Ir J Psych Med*, 18(2), 66-7.

Baudrillard, J. 1983. *Simulations*. New York: Semiotexte.

Baudrillard, J. 1998. *The Consumer Society: Myths and Structures*. London: Sage.

Bauman, Z. 2000. *Liquid Modernity*. Cambridge: Polity Press.

Bauman, Z. 2001. *The Individualized Society*. Cambridge: Polity Press.

Bauman, Z. 2002. *Society under Siege*. Cambridge: Polity Press.

Bauman, Z. 2005. *Liquid Life*. Cambridge: Polity Press.

Bauman, Z. 2007a. *Consuming Life*. Cambridge: Polity Press.

Bauman, Z. 2007b. *Liquid Times: Living in an Age of Uncertainty*. Cambridge: Polity Press.

Bauman, Z. and May, T. 2001. *Thinking Sociologically*. Oxford Blackwell.

Beardsworth, A. and Bryman, A. 1999. Late modernity and the dynamics of quasification: The case of the themed restaurant. *Sociological Review*, 47(2), 228-57.

Beaven, B. 2005. *Leisure, Citizenship and Working-Class Men in Britain, 1850-1945*. Manchester: Manchester University Press.

Bell, D. 2007. Cyberculture, in *Blackwell Encyclopedia of Sociology, volume 3 C*, edited by G. Ritzer. London: Blackwell Reference, available at: http://www.sociologyencyclopedia.com/public/book?id=g9781405124331_9781405124331 [accessed: December 2007].

Bennett, A. 1999. Subculture or neo-tribes? Rethinking the relationship between youth, style and musical taste. *Sociology*, 33(3), 599-617.

Bennett, A. 2005. *Culture and Everyday Life*. London: Sage.

Bennett, T. 2004. The invention of the modern cultural fact: Towards a critique of the critique of everyday life, in *Contemporary Culture and Everyday Life*, edited by E. Silva and T. Bennett. Durham: Sociology Press, 21-36.

Bennett, T. and Silva, B. 2004. Everyday Life in Contemporary Culture, in *Contemporary Culture and Everyday Life*, edited by E. Silva and T. Bennett. York: York Publishing Services, 1-20.

Benson, J. 1994. *The Rise of Consumer Society in Britain, 1880-1980*. London: Longman.

Ben-Zeev, A. 2000. *The Subtlety of Emotion*. Cambridge MA: MIT Press.

Berger, P. and Luckmann, T. 1967. *The Social Construction of Reality*. Harmondsworth: Penguin.

Blackshaw, T. 2002. The sociology of sport reassessed in light of the phenomenon of Zygmunt Bauman. *International Review for the Sociology of Sport*, 37(2), 199-217.

Blackshaw, T. 2008a. Politics, theory and practice: Contemporary theory and football. *Soccer & Society*, 9(3), 325-45.

Blackshaw, T. 2008b. Zygmunt Bauman, in *Key Sociological Thinkers, Second Edition*, edited by R. Stones. Basingstoke: Palgrave, 368-82.

Boden, D. and Molotch, H. 1994. The compulsion of proximity, in *Nowhere, Space, Time and Modernity*, edited by R. Friedland and D. Boden. Berkeley, CA: University of California Press, 257-86.

Bourdieu, P. 1977. *Outline of a Theory of Practice*. Cambridge: Cambridge University Press.

Bourdieu, P. 1978. Sport and social class. *Social Science Information*, 12(6), 819-40.

Bourdieu, P. 1984. *Distinction: A Critique of the Judgement of Taste*. London: Routledge.

Bourdieu, P. 1986. The Forms of Capital, in *Handbook of Theory and Research for the Sociology of Education*, edited by J.G. Richards. New York: Greenwood Press, 241-58.

Bourdieu, P. 1990. *The Logic of Practice*. Cambridge: Polity Press.

Bourdieu, P. 2002. The forms of capital, in *Readings in Economic Sociology*, edited by N.W. Biggart. Oxford: Blackwell, 280-91.

Bourdieu, P. 2003. *Firing Back against the Tyranny of the Market*. London: Verso.

Bourdieu, P. and Wacquant, L. 1992. *An Invitation to Reflexive Sociology*. Cambridge: Polity.

Boyle, R. and Haynes, R. 2000. *Sport, the Media, and Popular Culture*. Harlow: Pearson Education.

Boyle, R. and Haynes, R. 2004. *Football in the New Media Age*. London: Routledge.

Brailsford, D. 1991. *Sport, Time and Society: The British at Play*. London: Routledge.

Brick, C. 2001. Anti-consumption or New Consumption? Commodification, Identity and New Football, in *Leisure Cultures, Consumption and Commodification*, edited by J. Horne. Brighton: Leisure Studies Association, 3-16.

Briggs, A. 1968. *Victorian Cities*. Harmondsworth: Penguin Books.

Brown, A. 2008. Our club, our rules: Fan communities at FC United of Manchester. *Soccer & Society*, 9(3), 346-58.

Brown, A., Crabbe, T. and Mellor, G. 2008. Introduction – Football and community: Practical and theoretical considerations. *Soccer and Society*, 9(3), 303-12.

Bruyn, S.T. 2002. Studies of the mundane by participant observation. *Journal of Mundane Behaviour*, 3(2), available at: http://mundanebehavior.org/index2.htm. [accessed February 2012].

Bryman, A. 1993. The Disneyization of Society. *Sociological Review*, 47(1), 25-47.

Bryman, A. 2003. McDonalds as a Disneyized Institution: Global Implications. *American Behavioural Scientist*, 2(2), 154-67.

Bryman, A. 2004. *The Disneyization of Society*. London: Sage.

Bryman, A. 2008. *Social Research Methods, Third Edition*. Oxford: Oxford University Press.

Burdsey, D. 2007. *British Asians and Football: Culture, Identity and Exclusion*. London: Routledge.

Calhoun, D.W. 1987. *Sport, Culture, and Personality*. Champaign, IL: Human Kinetic Publishers.

Campbell, C. 1995. The Sociology of Consumption, in *Acknowledging Consumption: A Review of New Studies*, edited by D. Miller. London: Routledge, 96-126

Cashmore, E. 2000. *Making Sense of Sport*. London: Routledge.

Cavicchi, D. 1998. *Tramps like us: Music and Meaning amongst Springsteen Fans*. New York Oxford University Press.

Charmaz, K. 2006. *Constructing Grounded Theory: A Practical Guide through Qualitative Analysis*. London: Sage.

Cicourel, A. 1964. *Method and Measurement in Sociology*. New York: Free Press.

Clark, T. 2006. 'I'm Scunthorpe 'til I die': Constructing and (Re)negotiating identity through the terrace chant. *Soccer and Society*, 7(4), 494-507.

Clarke, J. and Critcher, C. 1985. *The Devil Makes Work: Leisure in Capitalist Britain*. London: Macmillan.

Clarke, J. 1978. Football and working class fans: Tradition and change, in *Football Hooliganism: The Wider Context*, edited by R. Ingham. London: Inter-Action, 37-60.

Clarke, J., Hall, S., Jefferson, T., and Roberts, B. 1976. Subcultures, cultures and class', in *Resistance Through Ritual: Youth Subcultures in Post War Britain*, edited by S. Hall and T. Jefferson. London: Hutchinson, 100-11.

Cleland, J. 2009. The changing organisational structure of football clubs and their relationship with the external media. *International Journal of Sport Communication*, 2(4), 417-31.

Cleland, J. 2010. From passive to active: The changing relationship between supporters and football clubs. *Soccer & Society*, 11(5), 537-52.

Coakley, J. 2008. *Sport in Society: Issues and Controversies, Seventh Edition*. Boston, MA: McGraw Hill.

Cohen, I. 1989. *Structuration Theory: Anthony Giddens and the Constitution of Social Life*. London: Macmillan.

Cohen, I. 2008. Anthony Giddens, in *Key Sociological Thinkers: Second Edition*, edited by R. Stones. Basingstoke: Palgrave, 323-38.

Collins, T. and Vamplew, W. 2000. The pub, the drinks trade and the early years of modern football. *The Sports Historian*, 1(20), 1-17.

Conn, D. 1997. *The Football Business*. Edinburgh: Mainstream.

Crabbe, T. 2008. Postmodern community and future directions: Fishing for community: England fans at the 2006 FIFA World Cup. *Soccer & Society*, 9(3), 428-38.

Crabbe, T. and Brown, A. 2004. You're not welcome anymore: The football crowd, class and social exclusion, in *British Football and Social Exclusion: Sport in the Global Society*, edited by S. Wagg. London: Routledge, 26-46.

Craib, I. 1992. *Anthony Giddens*. London: Routledge.

Crawford, G. 2001. Characteristics of a British ice hockey audience: Major findings of the 1998 and 1999 Manchester Storm Ice Hockey Club supporter surveys. *International Review for the Sociology of Sport*, 36(1), 78-81.

Crawford, G. 2002. Cultural tourists and cultural trends: Commercialization and the Coming of The Storm. *Culture, Sport, Society*, 5(1), 21-38.

Crawford, G. 2003. The career of the sport supporter: The case of the Manchester Storm. *Sociology*, 37(2), 219-37.

Crawford, G. 2004. *Consuming Sport: Fans, Sport and Culture*. London: Routledge.

Crawford, G. 2006. The Cult of Champ Man: The culture and pleasures of Championship Manager/Football Manager Gamers. *Information, Communication and Society*, 9(4), 496-514.

Crawford, G. 2007. Consumption of Sport, in *The Blackwell Encyclopedia of Sociology Volume 2*, edited by G. Ritzer. London: Blackwell Reference, 716.

Crawford, G. and Gosling, V.K. 2005. Toys for boys? Women's marginalization and participation as digital gamers. *Sociological Review Online*, 10(1). Available at: http://www.socresonline.org.uk/10/1/crawford.html. Accessed February 2012.

Crawshaw, P. 2004. The Logic of Practice in the Risky Community: The potential of the work of Pierre Bourdieu for theorising young men's risk-taking, in *Young People, Risk and Leisure: Constructing Identities in Everyday Life*, edited by W. Mitchell., R. Bunton. and E. Green. Basingstoke: Palgrave, 224-42.

Crawshaw, P. and Bunton, R. 2009. Logics of Practice in the Risk Environment. *Health, Risk and Society*, 11(3), 269-82.

Croll, A. 2000. *Civilizing the Urban: Popular Culture and Public Space in Merthyr, c.1870-1914*. Cardiff: University of Wales Press.

Crook, S. 1998. Minotaurs and other monsters: Everyday life in recent social theory. *Sociology*, 32(3), 523-40.

Cunningham, H. 1980. *Leisure in the Industrial Revolution. 1780-1880*. London: Croom Helm.

Dart, J. 2009. Blogging the 2006 Fifa World Cup Finals. *Sociology of Sport Journal*, 26(1), 107-26.

Davis, N. and Duncan, M. 2006. Sports Knowledge is Power: Reinforcing masculine privilege through fantasy sport league participation. *Journal of Sport and Social Issues*, 30(3), 244-64.

DeChristoforo, J. 2006. Everyday Life of a Sports Fan. *The Review of Communication*, 6(1-2), 163-5.

Denzin, N. 1989. *The Research Act*. New York: Prentice Hall.

Denzin, N. and Lincoln, Y. 2000. *Handbook of Qualitative Research*. Thousand Oaks CA: Sage.

Dixon, K. 2011. A third way for football fandom research: Anthony Giddens and Structuration Theory. *Soccer & Society*, 12(2), 279-98.

Dixon, K. and Flynn, D. 2008. Consuming "celebrated athletes": An investigation of desirable and undesirable characteristics. *Journal of Qualitative Research in Sport and Exercise*, 2(1), 13-29.

Douglas, M. 1966 [1992 reprint] *Purity and Danger: An Analysis of the Concepts of Pollution and Taboo*. London: Routledge.

Duke, V. 2002. Local Tradition Versus Globalisation: Resistance to the McDonaldisation and Disneyfication of Professional Football in England. *Football Studies*, 5(1), 5-23.

Dunning, E. and Curry, G. 2004. Public schools, status rivalry and the development of football, in *Sports Histories: Figurational Studies of the Development of Modern Sports*, edited by E. Dunning., D. Malcolm., and I. Waddington. New York: Routledge, 31-52.

Dunning, E. and Sheard, K. 1979. *Barbarians, Gentlemen and Players: A Sociological study of the Development of Rugby Football.* New York: New York University Press.

Dunning, E., Murphy, P., and Williams, J. 1988. *The Roots of Football Hooliganism: an Historical and Sociological Study.* London: Routledge.

Dunning, E., Murphy, P., and Waddington, I. 2002. Towards a sociological understanding of football hooliganism as a world phenomenon, in *Fighting Fans: Football Hooliganism as a World Phenomenon,* edited by E. Dunning., P. Murphy., I. Waddington and A. Astrinakis. Dublin: University College Dublin Press, 1-22.

Edensor, T. and Millington, S. 2008. 'This is Our City': Branding football and local embeddedness'. *Global Networks,* 8(2), 172-93.

Edwards, T. 2000. *Contradictions of Consumption: Concepts, Practices and Politics in Consumer Society.* Great Britain: St Edmundsbury Press.

Elias, N. 1939. [2000 reprint]. *The Civilizing Process.* Oxford: Blackwell.

Elias, N. and Dunning, E. 1986. *The Quest for Leisure and Excitement in the Civilising Process.* England, Basil: Blackwell.

Elliott, A. 2009. *Contemporary Social Theory: An Introduction.* London: Routledge.

Emmison, M. 2003. Social class and cultural mobility: Reconfiguring the cultural omnivore thesis. *Australian Journal of Sociology,* 39(3), 211-30.

Falcous, M. 1998. TV Made it all a New Game: Not again! A Case Study of the European Superleague. *Occasional Papers in Football Studies,* 1(1), 4-22.

Falk, P. 2007. Consumption experiential, in *The Blackwell Encyclopedia of Sociology, vol. 3. C.,* edited by G.Ritzer. London: Blackwell Reference. Available at http://www. sociologyencyclopedia.com/public/book?id=g9781405124331_9781405124331 . [accessed February 2011].

Fishwick, N. 1989. *English Football and Society: 1910-1950.* Manchester: Manchester University Press.

Fiske, J. 1992. The Cultural Economy of Fandom, in *The Adoring Audience: Fan Culture and Popular Media,* edited by L.A. Lewis. London and New York: Routledge, 30-49.

Flick, U. 2006. *An Introduction to Qualitative Research: Edition 3.* London: Sage.

Flick, U. 2009. *An Introduction to Qualitative Research: Edition 4.* London: Sage.

Football Task Force. 1999. *Football: Commercial Issues a Submission by the Football Task Force to the Minister of Sport.* London: The Football Task Force.

Forgacs, D. 1992. Disney animation and the basis of childhood. *Screen,* 33, 361-74.

Fort, R. and Quirk, J. 1995. Cross-subsidization, Incentives, and Outcomes in Professional Team Sports Leagues. *Journal of Economic Literature,* XXXIII, 1265-99

Foucault, M. 1979. *Discipline and Punish: The Birth of the Prison.* Harmondsworth: Penguin.

Furby, L. 1978. Possessions: Toward a theory of their meaning and function throughout the life cycle, in *Lifespan Development and Behaviour*, edited by P. Baltes. New York: Academic Press, 297-336.

Gabriel, Y. and Lang, T. 1995. *The Unmanageable Consumer: Contemporary Consumption and its Fragmentations*. London: Sage.

Gibbons, T. and Dixon, K. 2010. Surfs up!': A call to take English soccer fan interactions on the internet more seriously. *Soccer & Society*, 11(5), 599-613.

Gibbons, T. and Lusted, J. 2008. Is St. George enough? Considering the importance and displaying local identity while supporting the England National soccer team. *Annals of Leisure Research*, 10(5), 291-309.

Giddens, A. 1982. *Profiles and Critiques in Social Theory*. London: Macmillan Press.

Giddens, A. 1984. *The Constitution of Society*. Cambridge: Polity Press.

Giddens, A. 1990. *The Consequences of Modernity*. Cambridge: Polity Press.

Giddens, A. 1991. *Modernity and Self-Identity: Self and Society in the Late Modern Age*. Cambridge: Polity Press.

Giddens, A. 2009. *Sociology: 6th Edition*. Cambridge: Polity Press.

Giulianotti, R. 1999. *Football: A Sociology of the Global Game*. Cambridge: Polity.

Giulianotti, R. 2002. Supporters, followers, fans, and flaneurs: A Taxonomy of spectator identities in football. *Journal of Sport and Social Issues*, 26(1), 25-46.

Giulianotti, R. 2005. Sport spectators and the social consequences of commodification: Critical perspectives from Scottish football. *Journal of Sport & Social Issues*, 29(4), 386-410.

Goffman, E. 1968. *Asylums*. London: Penguin.

Goldblatt, D. 2010. *The Ball is Round: A Global History of Football*. London: Penguin.

Gratton, C. and Jones, I. 2010. *Research Methods for Sports Studies*. London: Routledge.

Gray, J., Sandvoss, C., and Harrington, L. 2007. Why study fans, in *Fandom Identities and Communities in a Mediated World*, edited by J. Gray., C. Sandvoss., and L. Harrington. New York: New York University Press, 1-16.

Grugulis, I. 2002. Nothing serious? Candidates use of humour in management training. *Human Relations*, 5(4), 387-406.

Guba, E.G. and Lincoln, Y.S. 1994. Competing paradigms in qualitative research, in *Handbook of Qualitative Research*, edited by N.K. Denzin and Y.S. Lincoln. Thousand Oaks: Sage, 105-17.

Guttmann, A. 1979. *From Ritual to Record*. New York: Columbia University Press.

Guttmann, A. 1986. *Sport Spectators*. New York: Columbia University Press.

Hamilton, R. and Bowers, B. 2006. Internet recruitment and e-mail interviews in qualitative studies, *Qualitative Health Research*, 16(6), 821-35.

Hammersley, M. and Atkinson, P. 1995. *Ethnography: Principles in Practice (second edition)*, Routledge: London.

Hand, D. 2001. City 'till I die? Recent trends in popular football writing. *Soccer & Society*, 21, 99-112.

Hargreaves, J. 1986. *Sport, Power and Culture: A Social and Historical Analysis of Popular Sports in Britain*. Cambridge: Polity Press.

Harris, C. 1998. Introduction: Theorizing fandom: Fans, subculture and identity, in *Theorizing Fandom: Fans, Subculture and Identity*, edited by C. Harris. New York: Hampton Press Inc, 3-8.

Hartley, J. 1999. *The Uses of Television*. London: Routledge.

Harvey, J. 2007. Sport and Social Capital, in *The Blackwell Encyclopedia of Sociology, vol. 3, S*, edited by G. Ritzer. London: Blackwell Reference: Available at: http://www.sociologyencyclopedia.com/public/book?id=g9781405124331_9781405124331 [accessed: December 2007].

Harvey, M., McMeedkin, A., Randles, S., Southerton, D., Tether, B., and Warde, A. 2001. Between demand and consumption: A framework for research. *CRIC Discussion Paper No 40. Centre for Research on Innovation and Competition:* The University of Manchester.

Hayward, K. and Yar, M. 2006. The 'Chav' phenomenon: Consumption, media and the construction of a new underclass. *Crime, Media, Culture*, 2(1), 9-28.

Hemingway, J. 1995. Leisure studies and interpretive social inquiry. *Leisure Studies*, 14(1), 32-47.

Henkoff, R. 1994. Finding, training and keeping the best service workers. *Fortune*, October 3, 52-8.

Hennion, A. 2007. Those things that hold us together: Taste and Sociology. *Cultural Sociology*, 1(1), 97-114.

Heritage, J. and Atkinson, J. 1984. Introduction, in *Structures of Social Action: Studies in Conversational Analysis*, edited by J. Atkinson and J. Heritage. Cambridge: Cambridge University Press, 1-17.

Hills, M. 2002. *Fan Cultures*. London and New York: Routledge.

Hills, M. 2007. Fans and Fan Culture, in *Blackwell Encyclopaedia of Sociology, vol3, F*, edited by G. Ritzer.London: Blackwell Reference. Available at: http://www.blackwellreference.com/subscriber/uid=71/tocnode?query=sport&widen= [accessed July 2007].

Hinch, T. and Higham, J. 2005. Sport, tourism and authenticity. *European Sport Management Quarterly*, 5(3), 243-56.

Hobsbawm, E. 1983. Introduction: Inventing Traditions, in *The Invention of Tradition*, edited by E. Hobsbawmn and T. Ranger. Cambridge: Cambridge University Press, 1-15.

Hochschild, A.R. 1983. *The Managed Heart*. Berkeley, CA: University of California Press.

Hoffmann, E. 2007. Open-ended interviews, power and emotional labour. *Journal of Contemporary Ethnography*, 36(3), 318-46.

Holt, R. 1990. *Sport and the British: A Modern History*. Oxford: Clarendon Press.

Hooker, J. 2003. *Working Across Cultures*. Stanford, CA: Stanford University Press.

Horne, J. 2006. *Sport in Consumer Culture*. Basingstoke: Palgrave.

Horne, J. and Jary, D. 2004. Anthony Giddens: Structuration Theory, and sport and leisure', in *Sport and Modern Social Theorists*, edited by R. Giulianotti. Basingstoke: Palgrave, 129-44.

Horne, J. and Manzenreiter, W. 2004. Football, Culture, Globalization: Why Professional Football has been Going East, in *Football Goes East: Business, Culture and the Peoples Game in East Asia*, edited by W. Manzenreiter and J. Horne. London Routledge, 1-17.

Horne, J., Tomlinson, A., and Whannel, G. 1999.*Understanding Sport: An Introduction to the Sociological and Cultural Analysis of Sport*. London: E&FN SPON.

Horton, E. 1997.*Moving the Goalposts: Football's Exploitation*. Edinburgh: Mainstream Publishing.

Horrie, C. 2002. *Premiership: Lifting the Lid on a Natural Obsession*. London: Pocket.

Howard, S. and Sayce, R. 2002. Branding, sponsorship and commerce in football. *Centre for the Sociology of Sport*, Factsheet 11. University of Leicester.

Huggins, M. 1989. The spread of Association Football in North East England, 1876-90: The pattern of diffusion. *The International Journal of the History of Sport*, 6(3), 298-318.

Hughson, J. 1999. A tale of two tribes: Expressive fandom in Australian soccer's A-league. *Culture, Sport and Society*, 2(3), 10-30.

Hughson, J. 2004. Sport in the "City of Culture: The Cultural Policy Connection. *International Journal of Cultural Policy*, 10(3), 319-30.

Hughson, J. 2009. Cultural history and the study of sport. *Sport in Society*, 12(1), 3-17.

Hughson, J. and Free, M. 2006. Paul Willis, Cultural Commodities, and Collective Sport Fandom. *Sociology of Sport Journal*, 23(1), 72-85.

Hughson, J., Inglis, D., and Free, M. 2005.*The Uses of Sport: A Critical Study*. London: Routledge.

Humphries, C. and Smith, A. 2006. Sports fandom as an occupation. Understanding the sport consumer through the lens of occupational science. *Int. J. Sport Management and Marketing*, 1(4), 331-48.

Hutchins, B., Rowe, D., and Ruddock, A. 2009. It's fantasy football made real: Networked media sport, the internet and the hybrid reality of my football club. *Sociology of Sport Journal*, 26(1), 89-106.

Illouz, E. 2009. Emotions, imagination and consumption: A new research agenda. *Journal of Consumer Culture*, 9(3), 377-413.

Ilmonen, K. 2004. The use of and commitment to goods. *Journal of Consumer Culture*, 4(1), 27-50.

Jary, D. 1999. The McDonaldization of sport and leisure, in *Resisting McDonaldization*, edited by B. Smart. London: Sage, 116-34.

Jenkins, R. 1992. *Pierre Bourdieu*. London: Routledge.

Jenkins, H. 2002. Interactive audiences? in *The New Media Book*, edited by D. Harries. London:BFI.

Johnes, M. 2007. We hate England! We hate England? National identity and anti-Englishness in Welsh soccer fan culture. *Unpublished Draft*. Available at: www.swan.ac.uk/history/staff/**johnes**/We%20Hate%20England.pdf.

Jones, I. 1997. Mixing qualitative and quantitative methods in sports fan research. *The Qualitative Report*, 3(4), Available at: http://www.nova.edu/ssss/QR/QR3-4/jones.html

Jones, I. 2000. A Mode of Serious Leisure Identification: The Case of Football Fandom. *Leisure Studies*, 19(4), 283-93.

Jones, K.W. 2008. Female Fandom: Identity, sexism and mens professional football in England. *Sociology of Sport Journal*, 1(25), 516-37.

Jones, S. 1986. *Workers at Play: A Social and Economic History of Leisure 1918-1939*. London: Routledge.

Katz, J.E., Rice, R.E., and Aspden, P. 2001. The Internet, 1995-2000: access, civic involvement and social interaction. *American Behavioural Scientist*, 45(3), 404-18.

King, A. 1997. The Lads: Masculinity and the new consumption of football. *Sociology*, 31(2), 329-46.

King, A. 1998. *The End of Terraces: The Transformation of English Football in the 1990s*. London: Leicester University Press.

King, A. 2011. The badge. *Soccer & Society*, 12(2), 74-75.

Kirchberg, V. 2007. Cultural Consumption Analysis: Beyond Structure and Agency. *Cultural Sociology*, 1(1), 115-36.

Klein, N.M. 1993. *Seven Minutes: The Life and Death of the American Animated Cartoon*. London: Verso.

Kraszewski, J. 2008. Pittsburgh in Fort Worth: Football Bars, Sports Television, Sport Fandom and the Management of Home. *Journal of Sport and Social Issues*, 32(2), 139-57.

Kuhn, T. 1970. *The Structure of Scientific Revolution, second edition*. Chicago, IL: University of Chicago Press.

Lasch, C. 1979. *The Degradation of Sport, the Culture of Narcissism: American Life in an Age of Diminishing Expectations*. New York: Norton and Company.

Lash, S. and Urry, J. 1994. *Economies of Signs and Space*. London: Sage.

Leonard, D.J. 2009. New media and global sporting cultures: Moving beyond the clichés and binaries. *Sociology of Sport Journal*, 26(1), 1-16.

Levermore, R. and Millward, P. 2007. Official policies and informal transversal networks: Creating 'pan-European identifications' through sport? *The Sociological Review*, 55(1), 144-64.

Lewis, R. 1997. The Genesis of Professional Football: Bolton-Blackburn-Darwen, the centre of innovation, 1878-85. *The International Journal of the History of Sport*, 14(1), 21-54.

Lincoln, E. and Guba, E. 1985. *Naturalistic Inquiry*. Beverly Hills: Sage.

Lloyd, G. 1988. *Aristotle: The Growth and Structure of his Thought*. Cambridge: Cambridge University Press.

Lofland, J. and Lofland, L.H. 1995. *Analysing Social Settings, Third edition*. Belmont, CA:Wadsworth.

Mahony, D.F., Madrigal, R. and Howard, D.R. 2000. Using the psychological commitment to team (PCT) scale to segment sport consumers based on loyalty. *Sport Marketing Quarterly*, 9(1), 15-25.

Malcolm, D., Jones, I. and Waddington, I. 2000. The people's game? Football spectatorship and demographic change. *Soccer and Society*, 1(1), 129-43.

Mangan, J. 1981. *Athleticism in the Victorian and Edwardian Public School: The Emergence and Consolidation of an Educational Ideology*. Cambridge: Cambridge University Press.

Mann, C. and Stewart, F. 2000. *Internet Communication and Qualitative Research: A Handbook for Researching Online*. London: Sage.

Martin, R., Puhlic-Doris, P., Larsen, G., Gray, J., and Weir, K. 2003. Individual differences in their use of humour and their relation to psychological well being: Development of the humour styles questionnaire. *Journal of Research in Personality*, 34(1), 48-75.

Mason, T. 1980. *Association Football and English Society 1863-1915*. Brighton: Harvester.

May, T. 1997. *Social Research: Issues, Methods and Processes, second edition*. Buckingham: Open University Press.

McCracken, G. 1986. Culture and Consumption: A theoretical account of the structure and movement of the cultural meaning of consumer goods. *Journal of Consumer Research*, 13(1), 71-84.

McCracken, G. 1991. *Culture and Consumption: New Approaches to the Symbolic Character of Consumer Goods and Activities*. Bloomington, IN: Indiana University Press.

McGill, C. 2001. *Football Inc. How Soccer Fans are Losing the Game*. London: Vision Paperbacks.

McLean, D. 1996. Leisure research and methodological pluralism: a response to Hemingway. *Leisure Studies*, 15(2), 137-41.

Mehus, I. 2010. The diffused audience of football. *Continuum: Journal of Media & Cultural Studies*, 24(6), 897-903.

Miles, S. 1998. McDonaldization and the Global Sports Stage: Constructing Consumer Meanings in a Rationalized Society, in *McDonaldization Revisited: Critical Essays on Consumer Culture*, edited by M. Alfino., J. Caputo., and R. Wynyard. Westport CT: Praeger publishers, 53-66.

Miles, M. and Huberman, M. 1994. *Qualitative Data Analysis: An Expanded Sourcebook*. London: Sage.

Miller, W. 1997. *The Anatomy of Disgust.* Cambridge MA: Harvard University Press.

Mills, C.W. 1959. *The Sociological Imagination.* New York: Oxford University Press.

Millward, P. 2006. We've all got the bug for Euro-Aways: What fans say about European Football Club Competition. *International Review for the Sociology of Sport,* 41(3/4), 375-93.

Moor, L. 2007. Sport and Commodification: A reflection on key concepts. *Journal of Sport and Social Issues,* 31(2), 128-42.

Morgan, J. 1994. *Leftist Theories of Sport: A Critique and Reconstruction.* Champaign, IL: University of Illinois Press.

Morreall, J. 1991. Humor and work. *Humor,* 4(3/4), 359-73.

Morrow, S. 1999. *The New Business of Football: Accountability and Finance in Football.* Basingstoke: Palgrave Macmillan.

Muggleton, D. 2000. *Inside Subculture: The Postmodern Meaning of Style.* Oxford: Berg.

Mullin, B., Hardy, S., and Sutton, W. 2000. *Sports Marketing.* Leeds: Human Kinetics.

Nash, R. 1997. Research note: concept and method in researching the football crowd. *Leisure Studies,* 16(2), 127-31.

Nash, R. 1999. Fan power: the FA Premier League, fandom and cultural contestation in the 1990s. *Unpublished PhD Thesis,* Department of Sociology, University of Liverpool.

Nash, R. 2000a. The sociology of English Football in the 1990s: Fandom, Business and Future Research. *Football Studies,* 3(1), 49-62.

Nash, R. 2000b. Contestation in Modern English Professional Football: The Independent Supporters Association Movement. *International Review for the Sociology of Sport,* 35(4), 465.

O'Neill, J. 1995. *The Poverty of Postmodernism.* London: Routledge.

Palmer, C. and Thompson, K. 2007. The paradoxes of football spectatorship: on-field and online expressions of social capital among the "Grog Squad". *Sociology of Sport Journal,* 24(3), 187-205.

Pascale, C. 2008. Common Sense and the Collaborate Production of Class. *Cultural Sociology,* 2(3), 345-67.

Payne, S. 2007. Grounded Theory, in *Analysing Qualitative Data in Psychology,* edited by E. Lyons and A. Coyle. London: Sage, 65-86.

Peterson, R. 1992. Understanding audience segmentation: from elite and mass to omnivore and univore. *Poetics,* 21(4), 243-58.

Peterson, R. 1997. The rise and fall of highbrow snobbery as a status marker. *Poetic,* 25, 75-92.

Peterson, R. 2005. Problems in comparative research: the example of omnivorousness. *Poetics,* 3(5), 257-82.

Peterson, R. and Simkus, A. 1992. How musical tastes mark occupational status groups, in *Cultivating Differences*, edited by M. Lamont and M. Fournier. Chicago, IL: University of Chicago Press, 152-86.

Pine, B.J. and Gilmore, J.H. 1999. *The Experience Economy: Work is Theatre and Every Business is a Stage*. Boston, MA: Harvard Business School Press.

Quick, S. 2000. Contemporary sport consumers: Some implications of linking fan typology with key spectator variables. *Sport Marketing Quarterly*, 9(3), 149-56.

Ray, L. 2007. Bauman's Irony, in *The Contemporary Bauman*, edited by A. Elliott. London: Routledge, 63-80.

Reckwitz, A. 2002. Toward a theory of social practices: A development in culturalist theorising. *European Journal of Social Theory*, 5(2), 243-63.

Redhead, S. 1993. *The Passion and the Fashion: Football Fandom in New Europe*. Aldershot: Avebury.

Redhead, S. 1997. *Post-Fandom and the Millennial Blues: The Transformation of Soccer Culture*. London: Routledge.

Redhead, S. 2000. *Repetitive Beat Generation*. Edinburgh: Rebel.

Rein, I., Kotler, P., and Shields, B. 2006. *The Elusive Fan*. Boston, MA: McGraw Hill.

Rheingold, H. 1993. *The Virtual Community: Homesteading on the Electronic Frontier*. Cambridge, MA: Addison-Wesley.

Rippon, A. 1981. *Great Soccer Clubs of the North East*. Frome. Butler and Tanner LTD.

Ritzer, G. 1993. *The McDonaldization of Society*. Thousand Oaks, CA: Pine Forge Press.

Ritzer, G. 1998. *The McDonaldization Thesis: Explorations and Extensions*. London: Sage.

Ritzer, G. and Stillman, T. 2001. The Modern Las Vegas Casino-Hotel: The Paradigmatic New Means of Consumption. *Management*, 4, 83-99.

Robbins, D. 2000. *Bourdieu and Culture*. London: Sage.

Robson, G. 2000. *No One Likes Us, We Don't Care: The Myth and Reality of Millwall*. Oxford: Berg.

Rodriguez, M. 2005. The place of women in Argentine football. *International Journal of the History of Sport*, 22(2), 231-45.

Rojek, C. 2004. The Consumerist Syndrome in Contemporary Society: An Interview with Zygmunt Bauman. *Journal of Consumer Culture*, 4(3), 291-312.

Ross, A. 1999. *The Celebration Chronicles: Life, Liberty, and the Pursuit of Property Value in Disney's New Town*. New York, NY: Ballantine.

Rowe, D. 1996. The global love-match: sport and television. *Media, Culture and Society*, 18(4), 565-82.

Rowe, D. 1999. *Sport, Culture and the Media: The Unholy Trinity*. Buckingham: Open University Press.

Rowson, S. 1934. A Statistical Survey of the Cinema Industry in Great Britain in 1934. *Journal of the Royal Statistical Society*, 99, 67-118.

Ruddock, A. 2005. Lets Kick Racism out of football – and the lefties too! Responses to Lee Bowyer on a West Ham web site. *Journal of Sport and Social Issues*, 9(4), 369-85.

Russell, D. 1997. *Football and the English*. Preston: Carnegie Publications.

Sage, G.H. 1998. *Power and Ideology in American Sport: A Critical Perspective, second edition*. Champaign, IL: Human Kinetics.

Sands, R. 2002. *Sport Ethnography*. Champaign, IL: Human Kinetics.

Sandvoss, C. 2003. *A Game of Two Halves: Football, Television and Globalization*. London: Routledge.

Sandvoss, C. 2005. Technological Evolution or Revolution? Sport Online Live Internet Commentary as Postmodern Cultural Form. *Convergence*, 10(3), 39-54.

Sayer, A. 1997. The dialectic of culture and economy, in *Geographies of Economics*, edited by R. Lee and J. Wills. London: Arnold.

Schatzki, T. 1997. Practices and Actions: A Wittgensteinian Critique of Bourdieu and Giddens *Philosophy of the Social Sciences*, 27(3), 283-308.

Schickel, R. 1986. *The Disney version: The Life, Times Art and Commerce of Walt Disney*. London: Pavilion.

Schmitt, B. and Simonson, A. 1997. *Marketing Aesthetics: The Strategic Management of Brands, Identity and Image*. New York: Free Press.

Scott, A.J. 2001. Capitalism, cities and the production of symbolic forms. *Transactions of the Institute of British Geographers*, NS, 26(1), 11-23.

Seal, C. 1998. Qualitative Interviewing, in *Researching Society and Culture*, edited by C. Seale. London: Sage, 202-16.

Seal, C. 1999. *The Quality of Qualitative Research*. Thousand Oaks: Sage.

Selwyn, N. 2004. Reconsidering political and popular understandings of the digital divide. *New Media & Society*, 6(3), 341-32.

Silverman, D. 2000. *Doing Qualitative Research: A Practical Handbook*. London: Sage.

Silverman, D. 2006. *Interpreting Qualitative Data, Third edition*. London: Sage.

Sloane, P.J. 1971. The Economics of Professional Football: The Football Club as a Utility Maximiser. *Scottish Journal of Political Economy*, 17 (June), 121-46.

Smart, B. 1999. Resisting McDonaldization, in *Resisting McDonaldization*, edited by B. Smart. London: Sage.

Smith, A. and Stewart, B. 1999. *Sports Management: A Guide to Professional Practice*. Sydney: Allen & Unwin.

Smith A. and Stewart, B. 2007. The Travelling fan: Understanding the mechanisms of sport fan consumption in a sport tourism setting. *Journal of Sport and Tourism*, 12(3/4), 155-81.

Smith, J.A. and Eatough, V. 2007. Interpretative phenomenological analysis, in *Analysing Qualitative Data in Psychology*, edited by E. Lyons and A. Coyle. London: Sage, 35-50.

SoB. *Sons of Ben Website*. [Online]. Available at: http://www.sonsofben.net/Home/Home.html [accessed February 2012].

Soja, E.W. 1989. *Postmodern Geographies: The Reassertion of Space in Critical Social Theory*. London: Verso.

Soja, E.W. 1996. *Thirdspace: Journeys to Los Angeles and other Real and Imagined Places*. Oxford: Blackwell.

Soja, E.W. 2000. *Postmetropolis: Critical Studies of Cities and Regions*. Oxford: Blackwell.

Solomon, M.R. 1998. Dressing for the part: The role of costume in the staging of the servicescape, in *Servicescapes: The Concept of Place in Contemporary Markets*. Lincolnwood, IL: NTC Business books, 81-108.

Spillman, L. 2007. Culture, in *The Blackwell Encyclopedia of Sociology, vol 3. C*, edited by G. Ritzer. London: Blackwell Reference, 924-5.

Spranger, E. 1928. *Types of Men: The Psychology and Ethics of Personality, Authorised Translation of the Fifth Edition*, Pigors, J.W. (Translator) Halle: M. Niemeyer. Available at: http://www.questia.com/PM.qst?a=o&d=98597744 [accessed December 2010].

Stewart, B. 1989. The nature of sport under capitalism and its relationship to the capitalist labour process. *Sporting Traditions*, 6(1), 322-32.

Stone, C. 2007. The Role of Football in Everyday Life. *Soccer & Society*, 8(2/3), 169-84.

Stones, R. 2005. *Structuration Theory*. Basingstoke: Palgrave.

Stuber, J. 2005. Asset or liability? The Importance of context in the occupational experience of upwardly mobile white males. *Sociological Forum*, 20(1), 139-66.

Sutton, W.A., McDonald, M.A., Milne, G.R., and Cimperman, A.J. 1997. Creating and fostering fan identification in professional sport. *Sports Marketing Quarterly*, 6(1), 15-29.

Sweetman, P. 2003. Twenty-first Century Dis-ease? Habitual Reflexivity or the Reflexive Habitus. *Sociological Review*, 51(4), 528-49.

Szymanski, S. and Kuypers, T. 1999. *Winners and Losers: The Business Strategy of Football*. London: Penguin.

Tabner, B. 2002. *Football through the Turnstiles … Again*. Bath: Bookcraft.

Taylor, I. 1971a. Soccer consciousness and soccer hooliganism, in *Images of Deviance*, edited by S. Cohen. Hamondsworth: Penguin, 163-4.

Taylor, I. 1971b. Football mad: A speculative sociology of soccer hooliganism, in *The Sociology of Sport*, edited by E. Dunning. London: Frank Class, 352-77.

Taylor, P. 1990. *Rt. Hon Lord Justice. The Hillsborough Stadium Disaster: Final Report*. London: HMSO.

Taylor, R. 1992. *Football and its Fans: Supporters and their Relationship with the Game 1885-1985*. Leicester: Leicester University Press.

Taylor, M. 2008. *The Association Game: A History of British Football*. London: Pearson Longman.

Thornton, S. 1995. *Club Cultures: Music, Media, and Subcultural Capital*. Cambridge: Polity.

Tischler, S. 1981. *Footballers and Businessmen: The Origins of Professional Soccer in England*. New York: Holmes & Meier.

Tomlinson, A. 1993. Culture of Commitment in Leisure: Notes towards the Understanding of a Serious Legacy. *World Leisure and Recreation Association Journal*, 35(1), 6-9.

Tomlinson, A. 2004. Pierre Bourdieu and the Sociological Study of Sport, in *Sport and Modern Social Theorists*, edited by R. Giulianotti. Basingstoke: Palgrave, 161-72.

Trienekens, S. 2002. Colourful distinction: The role of ethnicity and ethnic orientation in cultural consumption. *Poetics*, 30, 281-98.

Tuan, Y. 1974. *Topophilia*. Englewood Cliffs, NJ: Prentice Hall.

Turner, G. 2004. *Understanding Celebrity*. London: Sage Publications.

Turner, J.H. 1998. *The Structure of Sociological Theory*. Belmont, CA: Wadsworth Publishing.

Tyler, I. 2008. Chav Mum Chav Scum: Class disgust in contemporary Britain. *Feminist Media Studies*, 8(1), 17-34.

Ueno, T. 2003. Unlearning to Raver: Techno-party as the contact zone in trans-local formations, in *The Post-subcultures Reader*, edited by D. Muggleton and R. Weinzierl. Oxford: Berg, 101-17.

Vamplew, W. 1988. *Pay Up and Play the Game: Professional Sport in Britain 1875-1914*. Cambridge: Cambridge University Press.

Veblen, T. 1925. *The Theory of Leisure Class: An Economic Study of Institutions*. New York: Mentor.

Von Wright, G. 1971. *Explanation and Understanding*. Ithaca, NY: Cornell University Press.

Wacquant, L. 2008. Pierre Bourdieu, in *Key Sociological Thinkers second edition*. edited by R. Stones. Basingstoke: Palgrave, 261-77.

Waddington, I., Dunning, E., and Murphy, P. 1996. Research note: Surveying the social composition of football crowds. *Leisure Studies*, 15(1), 209-19.

Walz, G. 1998. Charlie Thorson and the temporary Disneyification of Warner Bros. cartoons. In *Reading the Rabbit: Explorations in Warner Bros. Animation*, edited by K.S. Sandler. New Brunswick, NJ: Rutgers University Press, 49-66.

Walvin, J. 1994. *The People's Game: The History of Football Revisited*. Edinburgh: Mainstream.

Wann, D.L. and Dolan, T.J. 1994. Attributions of highly identified sports spectators. *The Journal of Social Psychology*, 134(6), 783-92.

Wann, D.L., Melnick, M.J., Russell, G.W., and Pease, D.G. 2001. *Sports Fans: The Psychology and Social Impact of Spectators*. New York: Routledge.

Warde, A. 2004. Practice and Field: Revising Bourdieusian concepts. *CRIC Discussion Paper No.65*. Centre for Research on Innovation and Competition, University of Manchester. Available at: http://www.cric.ac.uk/cric/Pdfs/DP65. pdf [accessed October 2012].

Warde, A. 2005. Consumption and Theories of Practice. *Journal of Consumer Culture*, 5(2), 131-53.

Warde, A., Wright, D., and Gayo-cal, M. 2008. Dissecting the omnivorous in the UK.*Poetics*, 36(2-3), 119-45.

Warde, A. and Gayo-cal, M. 2009. The anatomy of cultural omnivorousness: The case of the United Kingdom. *Poetics*, 37(1), 119-45.

Wasko, J. 2001. *Understanding Disney: The Manufacture of Fantasy*. Cambridge: Polity.

Watts, M. 1999. Commodities, in *Introducing Human Geographies*, edited by P. Cloke., P. Crang and M. Goodwin. London: Arnold.

Webb, T., Schairato, T. and Danaher, G. 2002. *Understanding Bourdieu*. London: Sage.

Weber, M. 1968. *Economy and Society: An Outline of Interpretive Sociology*. New York: Bedminster Press.

Weed, M. 2006. The Story of an Ethnography: The experience of watching the 2002 World Cup in the Pub. *Soccer & Society*, 7(1), 76-95.

Weed, M. 2007. The Pub as a Virtual Football Fandom Venue: An Alternative to 'Being there'? *Soccer & Society*, 8 (2/3), 399-414.

Weed, M. 2008. Exploring the sport spectator experience: virtual football spectatorship in the pub. *Soccer & Society*, 9(2), 189-97.

Wellman, B. and Gulia, M. 1998. Virtual communities as communities: Net surfers don't ride alone, in *Communities in Cyberspace*, edited by M. Smith and P. Kollock. London: Routledge, 167-94.

Wellman, C. 2003. Do celebrated athletes have special responsibilities to be role models? An imagined dialog between Charles Barkley and Karl Malone, in *Sport Ethics: An Anthology*, edited by J. Boxil. Oxford: Blackwell, 333-6

Whannel, G. 1992. *Fields in Vision: Television Sport and Cultural Transformation*. London: Routledge.

Whannel, G. 2000. Sport and the Media, in *Handbook of Sports Studies*, edited by J. Coakley and E. Dunning. London: Sage, 291-308.

Whannel, G. 2009. Television and the transformation of sport. *The Annals of the American Academy of Political and Social Science*, 625(1), 205-18.

Wheaton, B. 2007. After Sport Culture: Rethinking Sport and Post-Subcultural Theory. *Journal of Sport and Social Issues*, 31(3), 238-307.

Wigglesworth, N. 1996. *The Evolution of English Sport*. London: Frank Cass.

Williams, C. 2005. *A Commodified World? Mapping the Limits of Capitalism*. London and New York: Zed Books.

Williams, J. 1995. FA Premier League Fan Survey: A National Survey of FA Premier League Club Fans, General Report. *Sir Norman Chester Centre for Football Research.* Leicester: Leicester University.

Williams, J. 1996. Surveying the social composition of football crowds: A reply to Waddington, Dunning and Murphy. *Leisure Studies*, 15(1), 25-19.

Williams, J. 1997. The 'New Football' in England and Sir John Hall's New 'Geordie Nation', in *Football and Regional Identity in Europe*, edited by S. Gehrmann. Munster: Lit Verlag.

Williams, J. 2006. Protect me from what I want: Football fandom, celebrity cultures and "new" football in England. *Soccer & Society*, 7(1), 96-114.

Williams, J. 2007. Rethinking Sports Fandom: The case of European Soccer. *Leisure Studies*, 26(2), 127-46.

Williams, J. and Hopkins, S. 2011. Over here: Americanization and the new politics of football club ownership: The case of Liverpool FC. *Sport in Society*, 14(2), 160-74.

Willis, P. 1979. *Learning to Labour: How Working Class Kids get Working Class Jobs.* New York: Columbia University Press.

Willis, P. 1990. *Common Culture: Symbolic Work at Play in the Everyday Cultures of the Young.* Milton Keynes: Open University Press.

Willis, P. 2000. *The Ethnographic Imagination.* Oxford: Polity.

Wilson, W. 2007. All together now, 'click': MLS soccer fans in cyberspace. *Soccer & Society*, 8 (2/3), 381-98.

Witzel, A. (2000). The problem centred interview. *Forum Qualitative Research*, 1. Available at: www.qualitative–research.net/fqs-texte/1-00/1-00witzel-e.htm.

Young, M. 1988. *The Metronomic Society: Natural Rhythms and Human Timetables.* Cambridge, MA: Harvard University Press.

Index